A COOKBOOK
FOR THE LEISURE YEARS

A Cookbook for the Leisure Years

WITH DIVIDENDS FOR YOU
OF MONEY, TIME AND ENERGY

Phyllis MacDonald

Doubleday & Company, Inc.   Garden City, New York

1967

LIBRARY OF CONGRESS CATALOG CARD NUMBER 67-19076
COPYRIGHT © 1967 BY PHYLLIS MACDONALD
ALL RIGHTS RESERVED
PRINTED IN THE UNITED STATES OF AMERICA
FIRST EDITION

To all who find these pages helpful
and in particular
to my "big" sister Georgene.

ACKNOWLEDGMENTS

It is not possible to thank personally by name all whose help brought this book to completion. Yet I would be remiss were I not to include here my especial thanks to a few.

The "Famous Beloved Americans" who so generously sent favorite menus and recipes.

Mr. Maurice Gold of the Morningside Health and Retirement Services who took the time to scan these pages and offer constructive suggestions.

Frank Prillo, the photographer-friend who gained the confidence of small black Dodo pictured on the jacket cover.

And Clara Claasen, senior cookbook editor, Doubleday and Company, Inc., whose support and encouragement were never failing.

PHYLLIS MACDONALD

FOREWORD

Miss MacDonald has developed an interesting and practical idea in preparing A COOKBOOK FOR THE LEISURE YEARS. Attractive and well-flavored food makes a substantial contribution to the enjoyment of life for nearly everyone, and this relationship increases when the years reach beyond the enormous appetite of youth. Tastes and preferences then tend to become more narrowly defined, and the search for elements of newness within preferred types of food adds to the enjoyment of cooking to please the individual.

In this instance the author has included an extra dividend by keeping an eye on the foods essential for good health. Without losing sight of the practical aspects of hospitality she has combined enjoyment with sound economy. Special occasions and special interest groups are identified to facilitate finding food suggestions that are likely to appeal.

Human interest for many cooks and consumers alike will be found among recipes and menus submitted by "Famous Beloved Americans," food "For Calorie Watchers," "Meals from a Table-Top Kitchen," and "Bargain Buys—An Exciting Hobby."

C. G. King

Charles Glen King, Ph.D.
President of the International
Union of Nutritional Sciences

March 6, 1967

CONTENTS

Recipes for items followed by an asterisk (*) can be found by consulting the Index.

A COOKBOOK
FOR THE LEISURE YEARS

*A book to help make retirement years
healthful, happy and productive.*

Chapter One

MORE MONEY, TIME AND ENERGY
FOR YOUR LEISURE YEARS

It is no longer newsworthy when men and women live twenty and more years after the normal retirement age of sixty-two or sixty-five. Almost all of us today have friends who travel abroad when they are well over eighty, or who start new, productive business ventures after retirement from lifelong professions. Now at last *you* are free to do exactly as you please, or you are counting the days until you will be your own boss. And how lucky you are to be retiring now! It is certainly fact, not fiction, that there was never a better time than right now to be over sixty.

Perhaps you are planning to stay in the home that has been home for many years. Or you may decide you have had enough of shoveling snow or sweeping up leaves. Literally thousands do seem to feel that way. Upon retirement they have sold the old home lock, stock and barrel to move into an apartment or one of the modern miracles called a retirement village. These complete small villages with their cheerful, individual homes or apartment accommodations are mushrooming all over the country, and prices vary to suit the pocketbook. It is not just the architects who concern themselves more and more with the needs of older citizens. The government, medical profession, churches, lodges, labor unions—all are actively planning for happy, healthful retirement years for the over-sixty group which currently numbers over nineteen million.

From now on, if you want to sleep late, who is to stop you? At last there is no time clock to punch, no dash to a crowded commuter train day after day after day, no endless deadlines, no bolted lunches. Your time is your own. You can do all of those things you had wanted to do if you only had the time. Take, for instance, that pile of clipped-out tempting recipes. If your collection is like most, it is coated with dust. Well, dust them off. You've time now to develop your culinary skills and to savor each tantalizing dish slowly to the last bite.

Of course no one can just sit back and take health and happiness for granted. To achieve our retirement goals—many healthful, active years ahead—let's be realistic and acknowledge that we can and must help ourselves. Doctors and nutritionists agree that the meals we consistently eat day after day play a major role in keeping our physical age below our chronological age and in increasing the years of active life we can enjoy.

The words calories, protein, vitamins, minerals are "old shoe" today to almost every retired homemaker. All know that it is the right food perhaps more than any other one thing that keeps us fit. At a price you can afford, meals planned intelligently will give you all of the essentials, with extras too—extras that make meals high spots in the day. Now that you have plenty of time to devote to meal planning and preparation, you'll find what an exciting hobby good meals that save dollars, time and energy can become. Before you know it, those saved pennies will add up to the price of some treat or extravagance you didn't think you could afford, such as a weekend trip, concert tickets, dozens of enjoyable extras. Minutes can be saved too, which might otherwise be wasted, simply by organizing a shopping list properly. Energy can be saved by taking advantage of your freezer or refrigerator freezing compartment.

Many of the menus and recipes which follow take into consideration supermarket bargain specials. The steps are given which will enable you to net substantial savings through proper storing and preparation. By cooking now and freezing part to serve days later, money, time and energy are saved. Large as some of these bargain buys may seem at first, meals will be varied and tasty to the last bargain bite.

One chapter gives you a great variety of recipes to use should soft foods be needed temporarily. Just because you may have a cold or are having dental repairs, there is no reason for you not to enjoy well-seasoned and attractive meals. In fact, these light-diet menus are so tempting you'll find yourself repeating them long after you are again fit as a fiddle. If overweight is your bugaboo and rich desserts an obsession, you'll find some unusually mouth-watering desserts with total calories unbelievably low.

The man "batching it" won't feel neglected either. There is one chapter just for him with gourmet meals he can serve with a flourish—meals guaranteed to make him the most sought-after host in the neighborhood. Why shouldn't he be? Aren't the best cooks often men? He has the time now to build up his own distinguished repertoire.

Of interest to everyone is a collection of menus and recipes contributed by beloved famous people. All of them your contemporaries, most are now enjoying their own leisure years. The letters which accompanied their prized recipes tell of hobbies newly discovered and rediscovered, herb gardens tended, time now for volunteer work. One writes: "Now we have the time for a long walk every day. It's the first time we've been able to make it a habit, and what an appetite it gives us."

You won't need quite as much food now that you aren't rushing around to make a living. Meals probably should be smaller, but there is never any retirement from the right foods eaten regularly *every day*. Skimping on essentials is no economy at all. It is the day-after-day nutritious meals that will make your friends say: "You look wonderful! I've never seen you look better! What are you doing to yourself?"

To help you plan these essentials into everyday meals,

here they are together with a few suggestions for making mealtimes the high spots in the day.

· *Every day* two servings of lean meat *or* poultry *or* fish *or* cheese *or* eggs.

· *Every day* one serving of citrus fruit *or* vegetable.

· *At least once a day* a dark green *or* yellow vegetable.

· *Daily, too,* a serving of potato *or* rice *or* macaroni *or* spaghetti.

· *Every day* two glasses of milk. Drink it as a beverage or "eat" it in puddings, soups, sauces, casseroles, etc. That milk can be whole milk, skim milk, buttermilk, nonfat dry milk solids, or evaporated milk—whichever suits your purpose. The protein and minerals will be the same, whichever form you choose.

· Have at least one hot food at every meal.

· Plan several days' menus at a time for economy in buying and to save time in food preparation.

· Eat in pleasant surroundings. No corner-of-the-drainboard for you. This does not mean a hard-to-iron tablecloth and napkins. There are dozens of perky, cheerful paper napkins and placemats to let you change your table scenery frequently.

· Let every meal contribute to your enjoyment of the day. Be a lazy eater. Take time to enjoy the bud in your bud vase. You have time now to appreciate the flavor and aroma of those herbs sprinkled into your savory ragout or bisque.

Chapter Two

BARGAIN BUYS—AN EXCITING HOBBY
HOW TO SHOP FOR FOOD BARGAINS
HOW TO KEEP THEM BARGAINS

For years, with the exception of some food shopping squeezed into busy Saturdays, most of us have had to shop the expensive way. More times than not haven't you hastily scribbled a list during the lunch hour, made a quick telephone call to the grocer, and hoped for the best? The extra nickels and dimes you knew this cost just had to be chalked off as a necessary evil. But now that you have more time you can save those nickels and dimes and serve better meals than ever before. What fun it will be to pick out your own peaches, the ones with the deep pink blush. You won't be the one now to eat the tomatoes that personal shoppers passed by. Now you can heft a few melons and take your pick.

Money isn't the only thing to consider, of course. Time, energy, nutritive value of foods, and personal preferences all are important. To avoid physical wear and tear, to say nothing of emotional irritation, keep a pad and pencil near the pantry shelf area. Jot down needed staples before they run out. Nothing can spoil the day faster than some forgotten essential in the recipe you are preparing. Scan supermarket ads for money-savers that can be worked into next week's menus. Plan at least three days', even a week's basic menus at a time.

The Time-saving Shopping List

• Organize needed purchases by categories. Group together staples, canned goods, baked goods, vegetables and fruits, meats, dairy products, frozen foods.

• Select foods in that order. Sugar and flour or canned beans don't change in quality from the market shelf to your own pantry shelf. Ice cream does. So buy the most perishable items last.

• Once home, reverse the order. Put ice cream and frozen foods away first. Breads can wait while you wash and store vegetables and fruits.

Are They Really Bargains?

No bargain is a bargain if eaten only because it was cheap. Family likes and dislikes come first. But even foods you do like and that seem like bargains may not be.

Canned and Packaged Foods: Fine print is hard to read, so take your glasses along when shopping. Then read that fine print carefully. By law ingredients must be listed on cans and most packages in the order of highest percentage. For instance, if a can of beef stew lists contents as Beef, Water, Carrots, etc., in that order, there is more beef in the can than anything else. It could be a real bargain, though priced ten cents higher than the can listing contents as Water, Carrots, Rice, Beef.

Eggs: The U. S. Department of Agriculture has this to say about grades: "U.S. AA and A grades of eggs are top quality, good for all uses, but most appreciated when poached, fried or cooked in the shell. U.S. B and C grades are fine, wholesome eggs, just as good for dishes in which appearance and delicate flavor are not so important." B and C grades are cheaper, of course. Use them in baked dishes, custards, sauces and salad dressings. For all purposes, their nutritive value is the same as that of their higher-priced grade A cousins. White and brown eggs have the same nutritive value too, though in some communities prices differ.

What Are the Best Meat Buys? As with eggs, grades of meat determine quality and flavor. Top grades have more fat throughout the muscle tissue and are more tender. For a company rib roast of beef or steak, of course you will splurge with the best and tenderest grade AA you can afford. But the more fat, the less actual protein. For stew, lean chuck of a B grade serves the purpose. Seasoned with herbs and vegetables, simmered until tender, it makes the right beef stew at substantially less than grade A.

Ground beef for hamburger may be priced as a seeming bargain, but it can run as high as 30 per cent fat. Ground lean chuck at over a dollar a pound is more economical when nutritive values are figured in terms of available protein.

Milk: For drinking purposes nothing compares with whole fresh milk. Yet can you tell the difference in muffins, gravy, etc., when nonfat dry milk, reconstituted with the right amount of water, is used? Can you honestly taste the difference if evaporated milk is substituted? Could be you have a good imagination. For pennies a quart, use nonfat dry milk or evaporated for all but drinking purposes. If you are in the process of losing pounds, the use of nonfat dry milk is preferable. If you whip it in a blender you'll find the flavor quite like that of fresh milk.

Butter or Margarine—Which? Flavor does differ in these two products, but not noticeably when used in cooking or even in such things as butter frosting.

Spices and Herbs: Treat yourself to fresh herbs when the season is right and freeze your surplus in plastic bags. Or buy them year-round in the tiny jars and packages. The packages are tiny for a very good reason. Ground spices and herbs lose much of their aroma and flavor within a few months, so the large bulk bargain isn't a bargain for any homemaker no matter how generous she is with herbs. To keep herbs and spices at their best longer, store them in a cool, dry place. Sorry—that cute spice rack right over the range isn't going to help the spices and herbs, pretty as it may make your kitchen.

Chili powder, cayenne, paprika, and curry powders, all products of dried, ground peppers of one sort or another, do best kept in the refrigerator.

Put Your Freezer to Work

A freezer can be one of your best friends and your faithful servant. It cuts down on shopping trips and on time and energy spent in food preparation. It can write your menu for you when you would rather keep on reading your book or spend the afternoon gardening. A true freezer is either a separate appliance with the internal temperature near zero, or a two-door refrigerator with one door opening separately into the freezing unit. If your freezer is the type with a freezing compartment in a one-door refrigerator—the type with a drop-door and holding tray beneath—it won't keep foods at the ideal zero, but it will keep them frozen. They may show some discoloration if held in this less-than-zero type much longer than a two-week period, so watch the dates of purchases a little more carefully than you might if you had a "true" freezer. A drop-door freezing unit will give a family of one or two plenty of opportunity to buy when the price is right for later use.

What Not to Freeze

Most foods can be frozen either as purchased or in ready-to-reheat prepared dishes. Notable exceptions are:

· Cottage and cream cheese, which tend to become watery or icy when frozen.

· Salad dressings and mayonnaise, except for the small amount of mayonnaise mixed into sandwich spreads, etc.

· Cooked egg whites, which toughen upon freezing.

· Salad greens and raw tomatoes.

· Frozen foods that have been defrosted. Bacterial growth or fermentation in such defrosted foods may be at a harmful level when refrozen and again thawed.

· Cooked potatoes. When freezing precooked stews or other combinations, omit potatoes. These often become soggy in the freezer. It is best to add half-cooked potatoes to the stew, then reheat until potatoes are tender.

How to Wrap and Store Foods for Freezing

Assuming that the foods you are going to freeze are good quality to begin with, no other single factor is as important as proper techniques in wrapping and the materials used.

· Wrap with moisture-proof freezer wrap designed for that purpose. Loss of moisture from foods tends to make them dry and tough and causes discoloration and loss of vitamins. You may prefer treated paper, clear plastic, foil or clear plastic bags. When using a sheet of freezer paper or plastic, make sure to use one large enough to allow at least one inch overlapping.

The "drugstore" wrap technique is a fine one for solid foods. Place food squarely in the center of the wrapping. Bring the front and back edges of the wrap up together over the food. Turn the edges under, making an inch fold, then fold the side edges down and under.

· Seal all edges with freezer tape so that no air can penetrate.

· Label and date each package, using a grease pencil or crayon for lettering.

· Or use clear vapor-proof plastic bags. These come in various sizes in convenient snap-off rolls. Fill them no more than two-thirds full. Twist the end of the bag, pressing out all of the air as you do. Fasten the bags with rubber bands.

· Moisture- and vapor-proof paperboard or plastic containers, as well as metal containers, are sold in any number of sizes. Some come with tight-fitting lids. Some have none. Many may be washed and re-used. Read package labels carefully to be sure of what you may expect from your container.

· And don't toss out your empty plastic ice cream containers! Wash them and save them for "free" food freezing containers.

· Relatively new and ideally designed for small portions of cooked casserole combinations are the small stainless steel and glass ovenware casserole dishes with snap-on plastic freezer caps. These snap-on caps are made to fit just as those used for cans of coffee or shortening. Cooked foods in these keep moistureproof and fresh without further sealing with freezer tape. When ready to reheat, just remove the plastic lid.

· Ovenware casseroles and dishes, as well as loaf pans, are convenient freezer containers for prepared foods which can be frozen cooked or uncooked. Heat them in their original containers. Such casseroles and pans do need to be wrapped and sealed before freezing. Even if they have lids to cover them in the freezer, they need this wrapping to make them moistureproof.

· Leave a half-inch "head space" when filling cardboard, metal or plastic containers with foods for freezing. All foods expand in freezing and such head space prevents containers from bursting.

· Check frequently on the dates marked on your foods. Store today's purchases to the back and rotate the older foods out first whenever consistent with the menu.

Freezing Fresh Vegetables

If you purchase some vegetables in quantity at a bargain price, cook enough today for dinner. In another kettle cook the rest only until about half done. Since freezing softens tissues, the time required to reheat completely cooked frozen vegetables would actually overcook them.

Then freezer-wrap completely cooled vegetables in quantities to serve at one meal or in individual serving packages.

Freezing Packages of Frozen Vegetables or Fruits

Ounce for ounce, the no-waste, no-work frozen vegetables and fruits are higher priced than such vegetables and fruits selected fresh at the peak of their season. But they aren't much higher when peelings and pits are considered. When your supermarket lists your favorites at an all-time bargain low, buy all that you can conveniently keep frozen.

If they are in a cardboard container and you know you will need the whole contents for one meal, freeze it as purchased. First look the box over for punctures or breaks. If you find one, overwrap with a sheet of freezer wrap and seal with tape.

If you need only part of a box at one meal, remove the contents in one frozen block. Dip a serrated knife in very hot water and cut the food into portions. Wrap portions for freezing individually.

Dry-pack plastic bags of frozen vegetables and fruits have points in their favor for the small family. They do away with sawing or cutting through blocks of frozen foods. They eliminate rewrapping. They are dry as marbles in their plastic bags, and you can pour out just what you need, press out the air again, and pop them back into the freezer. No labeling is needed, either, for these see-through bags.

Freezing Baked Foods

Most cakes, breads, rolls, cookies and pies seem to enjoy being frozen. Flavors in some actually improve.

Cakes and Frostings: Both homemade and bakery cakes with butter frosting (not the type with boiled frosting) freeze to give you fresh-as-ever cake when defrosted. Cut unused cake into individual slices. Wrap and freeze each separately. This slice-freezing is especially ideal for you who live alone. If you entertain often and know you will need a quarter or a half cake more often than the individual slices, then wrap cakes by the quarter or half before freezing.

If you are a cake-baking enthusiast, freeze unfrosted, completely cooled layers or loaves. Then ice the defrosted cake with your choice-of-the-moment frosting.

To prevent butter frosting from sticking to the freezer-wrapping material, place iced half cakes, quarters, or individual slices on a cookie sheet. Freeze just until the frosting is firm to the touch. Then wrap.

Rather than overload one cake, freeze dabs of unused butter frosting for later use. Such dabs may give you just enough for a cupcake or two for another meal.

Cookies: Whether home-baked or a surplus purchased when the price warranted stocking up, pack cookies carefully in a freezer container in layers. Separate each layer with a sheet of freezer wrap. Then overwrap and seal the container. If cookies are very tiny or fragile, lay them out on a cookie sheet and freeze them before wrapping. For the family of one or two, freeze a few cookies in a small container rather than in a large one that will be opened time after time.

Pies: Both baked and unbaked fruit pies, whether homemade or store-bought, freeze well. Chiffon or cream pies give less predictable, less consistent results. To be sure, it's best to make them just the day you want to serve them. Those living alone, even the family of two, may find it best to freeze half of a baked pie or individual pieces, as suggested for cakes. Freeze any leftover portion of a pie right in the pan just until firm. Then cut, wrap and freeze portions or individual pieces. By freezing until the juices are firm, handling is easy.

Bread: To serve fresh bread *always,* you can buy the little packaged half loaves, but these small loaves are not the most economical purchase. Large loaves can stay fresh too. Divide them in half and wrap each half for freezing. Or wrap together only a few slices, then freeze. You may want to do this especially when buying a variety of bread—white, whole wheat, rye, etc.

Many markets have a shelf of day-old bread and rolls at appreciable discounts. Nutritionally, these are just as good as their fresh-baked competitors. Use them for toast, toasted sandwiches and crumbs.

Freezing Cheese

With the exception of cream and cottage, cheese freezes well. Divide a large bargain into smaller units before freezing. All cheese tends to mold, even in the refrigerator. This is true especially after the original wrapping has been removed. But frozen cheese won't mold when properly sealed.

Freezing Butter or Margarine

These freeze well too. Buy by the pound to save money and to avoid running out before the next shopping trip.

Freezing Eggs

Which of us hasn't stored a few egg whites in a custard cup in the refrigerator expecting to use them soon. Days later we remembered them and had to throw them away. The same is true of yolks. Unless a recipe uses both whites and yolks at the same rate, these small leftovers seem a nuisance, too infinitesimal to bother saving. However, often one egg white, recently thrown away, is exactly what we need for the recipe at hand.

Whites: The easiest way to save whites in an identifiable individual form is to freeze them in individual muffin or custard cups—one white to each cup. When frozen solid, remove them from the pan by dipping it into warm water just as in unmolding a gelatin dessert. Store one or more hard-frozen whites in an airtight plastic container or in a tightly sealed plastic bag. Remove one or more as needed.

Yolks: Individual yolks aren't frozen as easily. They need to be broken and mixed with either sugar or salt before freezing. So freeze them by the quarter, half or whole cup. Beat them lightly with a fork to blend well. For each cup of liquid yolks add one tablespoon of corn syrup or sugar. Freeze them in airtight containers and use for baking. Or, instead of the sugar, add a half teaspoon of salt per cup. Then, when ready to use them, reduce the salt called for in the recipe accordingly.

If you have only one or two leftover yolks, why bother to freeze them? Store covered in the refrigerator and use them within twenty-four hours. Just don't forget. Use them in custard sauce, eggnog or added to a whole egg you are about to beat up and scramble.

Freezing Bits of This and That

• Chop any leftover bit of onion, green pepper, celery, or carrot. Wrap it in freezer material and freeze. You may save just the one tablespoon of chopped onion you need for some recipe—just enough green pepper without cutting into a fresh one. Add such bits to salads, sandwich mixtures, soups and casseroles.

• Save blobs of whipped cream too. Freeze leftover whipped cream, even just one tablespoonful. Drop it in dollops onto a small plate. Freeze unwrapped. When hard, put frozen blobs into a plastic container. Seal and freeze. What a time- and effort-saver these blobs can become when unexpected guests pop in. Or just for yourself when you have the strawberries but no cream.

Freezing Poultry

• If you freeze parts in the original container, double-wrap them in the original wrapped carton for extra protection. Sharp wing points or leg knuckles can puncture the tightly drawn wrapping if the packages are moved around in the freezer or stacked.

• Or remove chicken parts from the original container and wrap each part separately before freezing, especially if you plan to use parts one at a time.

• Wrap giblets separately.

• Don't stuff poultry before freezing. The length of time needed for freezing and defrosting can result in harmful bacterial growth in the middle of the stuffing.

· Remove stuffing from roasted poultry before freezing. Freeze it separately.

· To economize on freezer space, trim leftover chicken or turkey from the bones before packaging.

Freezing Fish

You aren't going to buy a quantity of fresh fillets. These you will buy as you need them, but you may have more shrimp from a pound than you want to use that day, or you might come back from a fishing trip loaded.

· Leave small raw fish whole. Clean them, blot them dry on paper towels and wrap individually before freezing.

· Cut larger fish into serving pieces first.

· Freeze shrimp either raw or cooked. Remove shells before freezing in order to conserve freezer space.

Freezing Meats

In the next chapter, with menus and recipes planned to give you the most for your money from supermarket weekend meat bargains, you'll find the freezing tips needed to keep them bargains to the last ounce.

Chapter Three

GILT-EDGED DIVIDENDS FROM
SUPERMARKET MEAT SPECIALS

That three-pound chunk of ground chuck looks like a lot of meat for your family of two, doesn't it? But at pennies off the regular price, grab it. Or buy two or three cut-up chickens—whatever the weekend meat special may be. The menus and recipes which follow keep them bargains to the last tasty bite. Some recipes are given in quantities to serve six in case you have a dinner party in mind. But you don't have to wait for company. Prepare for the six, then divide the six servings in thirds. Eat one third today and freeze each of the other thirds separately to reheat and serve when a matinee or bridge club takes most of the day. With these menus you won't be eating the same old pot roast day after day after day. Your surplus turns into such gourmets' delights as beef stroganoff, ragout of beef, and hash fit for the President.

THE THREE-POUND GROUND CHUCK BARGAIN

To keep it a bargain, divide it into patties of about four ounces each. At four ounces each you'll have twelve as near the same size as you can estimate. Then wrap each separately for freezing. Or stack them with moistureproof paper between each patty. Why bother to do this? You'll find out if you already haven't. Have you ever frozen even one pound of ground beef in a solid chunk? Samson himself couldn't have cut it into patties! It had to defrost at least partially before you could do a thing with it. Once thawed, all had to be

cooked then and there. (Thawed meat can't be safely refrozen. Harmful bacteria may develop during the defrosting
and refreezing process.) You ate ground beef in some form
or other until it seemed you couldn't face ground beef again.
Or Rover had more than his share.

With the four-ounce patty you cinch your bargain. These
patties are "negotiable." Four of them make a pound. If
your recipe calls for half a pound of ground beef, remove
two from the freezer, etc. Now for the menus and recipes.

Apple Juice or Cider Cocktail
Baked Stuffed Burgers with Mushroom Sauce*
Fluffy Baked Potatoes
Braised Celery and Tomatoes*
Buttered Rolls
Deep-Dish Apple Scallop for Two*
Tea or Coffee or Milk

Three-Meal Meat Loaf with Crunchy Carrot Gravy*
Mashed Potatoes
Your Choice of Vegetable
Tomato Salad
Melba Toast or Rolls
Ambrosia*
Tea or Coffee or Milk

Fruit Cocktail
Fifteen-Minute Meatballs in Tomato Sauce*
Steamed Rice
Buttered Green Beans
Mixed Pickles   Olives
Buttered Rolls
Raspberry Refrigerator Pudding*
Tea or Coffee or Milk

Deviled Hamburger Puffs*
Creamy Succotash*
Peach and Cottage Cheese Salad
Ice Cream   Cookies
Tea or Coffee

BAKED STUFFED BURGERS WITH
MUSHROOM SAUCE

½ pound ground lean chuck
    (2 4-ounce frozen
    patties, defrosted)
Salt
1 slice packaged American
    cheese

2 thin slices of onion
About half of a 10½-ounce
    can of undiluted
    condensed cream of
    mushroom soup[1]
Chopped parsley

Shape beef into 4 thin patties, each about 4 inches in diameter. Sprinkle them lightly with salt. Cut cheese in half. Place a piece of cheese and a slice of onion on 2 of the patties. Top sandwich-style with remaining patties. Arrange burgers in a shallow baking dish. Heat oven to 400° F. Bake burgers in preheated oven for 15 minutes. Beat soup until smooth. Pour it over the patties. Continue to bake until sauce is hot, about 5 or 6 minutes longer. Serve sprinkled with chopped parsley. Makes 2 servings.

[1] Refrigerate leftover soup. Enough for a cup of soup for 2, it may be served for lunch tomorrow.

BRAISED CELERY AND TOMATOES

½ tablespoon butter,
margarine or bacon
drippings
2 outer ribs of celery, cut
in ½-inch slices

1 peeled medium-sized
tomato
½ teaspoon dry onion flakes
⅛ teaspoon salt
Dash pepper
⅔ cup boiling water

Melt butter in a small saucepan with a cover. Add remaining ingredients. Bring to a boil; reduce heat; cover and simmer 5 minutes. Remove cover and continue to cook over medium heat, stirring occasionally, until moisture is absorbed. Makes 2 servings.

DEEP-DISH APPLE SCALLOP FOR TWO

TOPPING

2 tablespoons all-purpose flour
1 tablespoon brown sugar, packed
1 tablespoon soft butter or margarine

FILLING

3 medium-sized tart apples
1 teaspoon lemon juice
2 teaspoons flour
¼ cup sugar

Dash salt
¼ teaspoon ground cinnamon
Dash ground nutmeg

Heat oven to 400° F. For the topping combine flour, brown sugar and butter until crumbly. Chill it while preparing filling. Core and peel apples. Slice them thinly into a bowl. Sprinkle with lemon juice. Combine flour, sugar, salt, cinnamon, and nutmeg. Add mixture to apples and toss lightly to coat them well. Turn into a 2-cup baking dish and sprinkle with the topping. Bake 35 to 40 minutes in preheated oven or until apples are tender. Serve warm or chilled. Makes 2 generous servings.

THREE-MEAL MEAT LOAF WITH CRUNCHY CARROT GRAVY

THE MEAT LOAF

1 pound ground lean beef
  (4 4-ounce frozen patties,
  defrosted)
1 tablespoon finely chopped
  onion
2 tablespoons chopped
  parsley or 1 teaspoon
  dry parsley flakes

½ teaspoon salt
⅛ teaspoon pepper
1 teaspoon ground thyme
1 tablespoon chili sauce
1 cup quick-cooking oats
⅓ cup milk
1 egg, lightly beaten

Heat oven to 350° F. In a large bowl, blend all ingredients. Shape meat mixture into a loaf and place it in an ungreased 9- by 5-inch loaf pan. Bake in preheated oven for 1 hour. Serve with Crunchy Carrot Gravy, below. Cut two slices from the leftover cold meat loaf for sandwiches tomorrow. Then wrap and freeze the rest for another meal.

CRUNCHY CARROT GRAVY

Drippings from the meat
  loaf pan
2 teaspoons flour
Dash salt

Dash pepper
⅔ cup milk
¼ cup shredded carrots

Pour drippings from the meat loaf pan into a small skillet. Measure flour, salt and pepper into a small bowl. Stir in milk, blending well. Pour mixture into drippings. Cook over medium heat, stirring constantly, until gravy thickens. Add carrots and serve with meat loaf.

AMBROSIA

1 orange, peeled and sliced　　*2 tablespoons shredded*
1 banana, sliced　　　　　　　　*moist coconut*
1 tablespoon sugar

Half an hour before dinner, combine all ingredients and chill. Makes 2 servings.

FIFTEEN-MINUTE MEATBALLS
IN TOMATO SAUCE

1 pound lean ground beef　　　*1 tablespoon chopped*
　(4 4-ounce frozen patties,　　　*parsley or 1 teaspoon dry*
　defrosted)　　　　　　　　　　*parsley flakes*
¾ teaspoon salt　　　　　　　*1 1-pound can vegetable*
¼ teaspoon pepper　　　　　　　*juice cocktail*
　　　　　　　　　　　　　　　Fluffy steamed rice

In a bowl blend beef, salt, pepper and parsley well. Form mixture into little balls about the size of walnuts. In a large skillet heat the vegetable juice cocktail to boiling. Add meatballs. Turn heat low and cook 12 to 15 minutes, basting meatballs occasionally with the sauce in the pan. The sauce will thicken until it is about the consistency of cream gravy. Serve half over fluffy rice for today's dinner. Cool the rest completely and freeze for another meal. Makes 4 servings.

RASPBERRY REFRIGERATOR PUDDING

6 *packaged vanilla wafers*
1 *tablespoon raspberry*
  jelly

1 *package instant vanilla*
  pudding mix
1½ *cups milk*

Spread the vanilla wafers with the jelly. Place 1 spread wafer in the bottom of each of 3 custard cups. Blend together the pudding and milk, beating as the package directs. Pour ⅓ of the pudding into each custard cup. Let stand 1 minute. Top each with 1 of the remaining spread wafers. Chill. Makes 3 servings—2 for dinner, 1 for a bedtime snack for the one who gets it first.

DEVILED HAMBURGER PUFFS

1 *teaspoon dry onion flakes*
½ *teaspoon salt*
½ *teaspoon dry mustard*
¼ *teaspoon baking powder*
⅛ *teaspoon pepper*

⅛ *teaspoon ground allspice*
½ *pound ground lean chuck*
2 *eggs, separated*
Chili sauce

Combine onion, salt, mustard, baking powder, pepper and allspice. Sprinkle the mixture over the beef in a bowl and mix to blend well. Blend in egg yolks. Beat egg whites until they stand in soft peaks. Fold them into the beef mixture. Drop by tablespoonfuls into a greased heavy skillet. Cook over low heat until well puffed over the top and browned underneath. With a pancake turner turn them to brown the other side. Serve with chili sauce. Makes 2 servings with a small second helping for the hungrier one.

CREAMY SUCCOTASH

Frozen baby limas (¼ of a
    10-ounce package)
1 8-ounce can cream-style
    corn
¼ teaspoon salt

Dash pepper
2 teaspoons butter or
    margarine
1 teaspoon finely chopped
    chives

Cook frozen limas in boiling salted water to cover for 15 minutes or until tender. Drain well. Add remaining ingredients and heat, stirring over low heat just until steaming hot. Makes 2 generous servings.

THE BIG POT ROAST BARGAIN

Who objects to a second meal from a mouth-watering pot roast? Often the flavors the second time around seem even more mellow and tantalizing than the first. But a three- or four-pound bargain-buy of pot roast doesn't have to be served again and again as pot roast. Here are the menus and recipes to prove the point. Prepare it first for some gala occasion as Old-Fashioned Pot Roast of Beef with Vegetables.* Then use your surplus for three different as can be meals such as: Beef Stroganoff,* Beef and Vegetable Pie with Mashed Potato Border* and the yummiest Roast Beef Hash* you ever ate.

Chicken Noodle Soup
Old-Fashioned Pot Roast of Beef with Vegetables*
Watermelon Pickles
Baking Powder Biscuits
Celery Sticks and Olives
Baked Stuffed Fresh Pears*
Tea or Coffee or Milk

Tomato Juice Cocktail
Beef Stroganoff with Poppy-Seed Noodles*
Buttered Green Beans
Tossed Salad Melba Toast
Plum Duff*
Tea or Coffee or Milk

Beef and Vegetable Pie with
Mashed Potato Border*
Coleslaw
Corn Muffins—Your Own or Packaged
Chocolate Icebox Cake*
Tea or Coffee

Roast Beef Hash with Poached Eggs*
Spicy Marmalade Beets*
Hearts of Lettuce Russian Dressing
Blueberry-Lemon Crumble*
or Your Favorite Ice Cream
Tea or Coffee or Milk

OLD-FASHIONED POT ROAST OF BEEF
WITH VEGETABLES

*3½- to 4-pound pot roast of
    beef*
*2 tablespoons all-purpose
    flour*
1 teaspoon salt
*1 tablespoon bacon
    drippings or vegetable oil*
6 peppercorns

1 bay leaf
1 cup water
*¼ cup frozen diced green
    pepper*
*2 medium-sized carrots,
    scraped*
*2 medium-sized onions,
    peeled*

Wipe the roast with damp paper towels. Blend together
the flour and salt and rub them into the surface of the roast.
In a Dutch oven heat the drippings or oil; add the roast and
brown it well on all sides. Add the peppercorns, bay leaf
and water. Cover and simmer 1¼ hours, adding more water
from time to time to keep ½ to 1 inch liquid in the bottom
of the Dutch oven. Add vegetables; cover and simmer 45
minutes or until the roast and vegetables are tender. Remove
the roast and vegetables to a hot platter. Keep warm.

FOR THE GRAVY

Liquid from pan
Hot water
¼ cup all-purpose flour

½ cup cold water
Salt and pepper to taste

To make the gravy, strain the liquid in the pan through a
coarse sieve. Add enough hot water to make 2½ cups liquid.
Return it to the Dutch oven. Blend the flour and cold water
to a smooth paste. Slowly stir it into the liquid in the pan.

Bring to a boil, stirring constantly. Reduce heat. Simmer 4 to 5 minutes, or until gravy is as thick as you like it. Season to taste with salt and pepper. Makes about 2½ cups.

Serve as much gravy as you need with your first pot roast dinner. Then freeze what is left, dividing it about equally into two plastic containers. Each container will have about ¾ cup—enough to use later with the Stroganoff* and the Beef and Vegetable Pie.*

For the magic wand technique that makes your leftover pot roast add up exactly to the amounts needed in the rest of your leftover pot roast recipes, cut off and wrap together two ½-inch slices for the Stroganoff. Freeze it till the day you plan to serve Stroganoff. Divide the rest in half. Wrap and freeze each half separately. One makes the Beef and Vegetable Pie, one the Roast Beef Hash.*

BAKED STUFFED FRESH PEARS

2 medium-sized firm, fresh pears	Dash cinnamon
½ teaspoon grated orange rind	2 tablespoons sugar
	¼ cup water
	¼ cup orange juice
2 coarsely crumbled packaged fig bars	1 tablespoon honey

Heat oven to 400° F. Wash and peel the pears. Cut them in half lengthwise and remove the cores. In a small bowl blend together orange rind, fig bar crumbs and cinnamon. Sprinkle about ½ teaspoon of the sugar into each cavity where cores were removed. Stuff cavities with fig stuffing and press two halves back together. Arrange the stuffed pears in a small baking dish. In a saucepan combine the remaining sugar, water, orange juice and honey. Bring the mixture to a boil, stirring until the sugar is dissolved. Pour over the pears. Bake in preheated oven 30 to 40 minutes, or until tender, basting occasionally with the orange syrup from the pan. Makes 2 servings.

BEEF STROGANOFF WITH POPPY-SEED NOODLES

THE STROGANOFF

2 slices defrosted leftover cooked pot roast

2 tablespoons butter, margarine or vegetable oil

1 4-ounce can sliced mushrooms

1 medium-sized onion, thinly sliced

½ teaspoon dried dill weed

About ¾ cup Pot Roast Gravy,* defrosted (left from the original pot roast)

½ cup commercial sour cream

Salt

Pepper

Cut roast beef slices in ½-inch strips. Heat butter in a medium-sized saucepan. Brown beef lightly in the butter. Drain mushrooms, reserving the liquid. Add mushrooms, along with the sliced onion, to the beef. Cook over medium heat until all are lightly browned. Add mushroom liquid and dill. Simmer, uncovered, for about 4 minutes or until the liquid in the pan is almost all absorbed. Stir in the gravy. Heat to boiling. Remove from heat. Stir in sour cream. Season to taste with salt and pepper. Serve over Poppy-Seed Noodles. Makes 2 servings.

POPPY-SEED NOODLES

1 quart water

1 teaspoon salt

2 cups packaged noodles

1 tablespoon melted butter or margarine

1 teaspoon poppy seeds

In a saucepan bring water and salt to a boil. Sprinkle in noodles and cook over medium heat, uncovered, for 9 minutes or until noodles are tender. Drain well in a colander or sieve. Toss them with melted butter and poppy seeds. Serve with Beef Stroganoff. Makes 2 servings.

PLUM DUFF

4 fresh plums (about ½ pound)
2 tablespoons sugar
Dash grated nutmeg
⅓ cup biscuit mix
2 teaspoons sugar

2 teaspoons melted butter or margarine
2 tablespoons milk
½ teaspoon sugar, blended with a dash of ground cinnamon

Heat the oven to 350° F. Cut plums in half; remove pits and slice into 2 custard cups. Sprinkle a tablespoon of the sugar over the plums in each cup. Sprinkle with nutmeg. In a small bowl combine the biscuit mix, 2 teaspoons sugar, melted butter and milk. Stir to blend well. Spoon batter over plums. Then sprinkle with cinnamon sugar. Bake in preheated oven for 30 minutes or until bubbling hot and lightly browned. Makes 2 servings.

BEEF AND VEGETABLE PIE WITH MASHED POTATO BORDER

2 tablespoons vegetable oil or bacon drippings

About 1½ cups defrosted leftover Pot Roast of Beef,* cut in 1-inch cubes

2 tablespoons grated onion

1 rib of celery, finely diced

½ cup tomato juice or water

1 cup cooked fresh or frozen mixed peas and carrots

¾ cup Pot Roast Gravy,* defrosted

Salt and pepper to taste

Packaged instant mashed potatoes

1 teaspoon melted butter or margarine

Paprika

Heat oil or drippings in a heavy medium-sized saucepan. Add beef, onion and celery. Cook over low heat until vegetables are beginning to brown. Add tomato juice or water. Cover and simmer 2 to 3 minutes or until celery is tender. Stir in peas and carrots and gravy. Heat just to boiling. Season to taste with salt and pepper.

Prepare two servings of instant mashed potatoes, following the instructions given on the package. Ladle beef and vegetables into individual ramekins. Make a border of mashed potatoes around the edge of each. Drizzle potatoes with melted butter and sprinkle with paprika. Makes 2 servings.

CHOCOLATE ICEBOX CAKE

½ cup heavy cream

¼ teaspoon vanilla extract

10 packaged chocolate icebox wafers

Whip cream until stiff. Stir in vanilla. Spread each wafer with whipped cream. Stack spread wafers. Turn the stack on its side on a serving plate and press it together to form a cylinder of cookies with cream between. Spread the top and sides with the rest of the whipped cream. Chill at least 3 hours or overnight. Slice in diagonal slices. Makes 2 to 3 servings.

ROAST BEEF HASH WITH POACHED EGGS

About 1 cup finely chopped cooked Pot Roast of Beef*

1¼ cups finely chopped cooked cold potatoes

1 tablespoon chopped green pepper

2 tablespoons finely chopped onion

¼ teaspoon salt

½ teaspoon Worcestershire sauce

2 tablespoons beef gravy or milk

2 tablespoons vegetable oil or bacon drippings

2 poached eggs

Paprika or chopped parsley

In a medium-sized bowl combine beef, potatoes, green pepper, onion, salt, Worcestershire sauce and gravy. Toss to blend well. Heat oil in an 8-inch skillet. Spread hash over the bottom of the skillet and cook over low heat until steaming hot and most of the liquid is absorbed (about 10 minutes). Turn hash over occasionally with a pancake turner to stir in the browned bits on the bottom. Cover and cook about 10 minutes longer or until brown and crusty on the bottom. Serve each portion topped with a poached egg and sprinkled with paprika or parsley. Makes 2 servings.

SPICY MARMALADE BEETS

2 tablespoons sugar
½ tablespoon cornstarch
Dash salt
⅛ teaspoon ground cloves
¼ teaspoon ground
  cinnamon
2 tablespoons cider vinegar

¼ cup water
1 tablespoon butter or
  margarine
2 tablespoons orange
  marmalade
1 to 1½ cups canned sliced
  beets, well drained

Combine sugar, cornstarch, salt, spices, vinegar and water in a small saucepan. Cook, stirring constantly, until sauce is smooth and thickened. Stir in butter and marmalade. Add beets. Cover and heat slowly for a minute or two or until beets are piping hot. Makes 2 generous servings.

BLUEBERRY-LEMON CRUMBLE

1 cup fresh blueberries (or
  the frozen, dry-pack,
  unsweetened)
1½ tablespoons lemon
  juice
1 cup leftover cake, cut in
  ½-inch cubes, or packaged
  pound cake cubes

3 tablespoons brown sugar,
  packed
3 tablespoons sugar
2 tablespoons water
½ teaspoon grated lemon
  rind
Milk or light cream

Heat oven to 350° F. If using fresh berries, wash and drain them well. Arrange them in the bottom of a 2-cup baking dish. Sprinkle with the lemon juice and cake cubes. In a small saucepan combine all the remaining ingredients except milk. Bring mixture to a boil, stirring constantly.

Pour over the cake cubes. Bake in preheated oven about 20 to 25 minutes or until bubbling hot. Serve warm with milk or cream. Or use 2 dollops of frozen whipped cream if you are lucky enough to have some on hand. (Frozen dabs of leftover whipped cream are discussed in Chapter Two.) Makes 2 generous servings.

CHICKEN PARTS—TOPS IN BARGAINS

For a festive dinner-party-on-a-budget, buy chicken packaged to suit every preference. Plump breasts for those who never touch dark meat, and drumsticks and thighs for the dark meat advocates! Aren't we lucky that our most popular company fare is also the most inexpensive, and that we can serve it in so many dozens of varied, tasty dishes. The chicken recipes to serve six in the menus which follow can all be prepared ahead of time. Tuck them away in your freezer to give you a work-free evening with your guests. But you don't have to wait for a dinner party. Eat what you need today and freeze the rest in individual portions to save the day days later when you have a yen for chicken and no time to prepare it.

Jellied Consommé with Lemon Wedges
Chicken Breasts in Orange Sauce*
Mashed Sweet Potatoes
Buttered Broccoli and Mushrooms
Marinated Artichoke-and-Tomato Salad*
Hot Dinner Rolls   Butter or Margarine
Graham Cracker Meringue Shell à la Mode*
Tea or Coffee

Fresh Fruit Cup
Chicken Paprika*
Tiny Parsley Potatoes
Buttered Peas and Pearl Onions
Celery Hearts Carrot Sticks Olives
Buttered Rolls Melba Toast
Mocha Pudding Pie*
Tea or Coffee or Milk

Baked Sesame Chicken*
Rice Pilaf*
Buttered Green Vegetable
Tossed Salad
Buttered Brown-and-Serve Croissants
Assorted Crackers and Cheese Fresh Grapes
Tea or Coffee

CHICKEN BREASTS IN ORANGE SAUCE

3 large whole chicken breasts, split	½ teaspoon grated orange rind
¼ cup all-purpose flour	1 cup orange juice
1 teaspoon salt	¼ cup water
Dash pepper	1 tablespoon instant minced onion
¼ cup butter or margarine	
1 tablespoon sugar	1 teaspoon crushed rosemary leaves
1 teaspoon cornstarch	

Heat oven to 375° F. Wipe chicken breasts with damp paper towels. In a clean paper bag combine flour, salt and pepper. Shake chicken breasts a few at a time in the flour mixture, coating each piece well. Heat butter in a Dutch oven or heavy skillet. Add chicken pieces and brown them well on all sides. Remove them to a shallow baking pan.

In a small saucepan blend sugar, cornstarch, orange rind, orange juice, water, onion and rosemary. Cook, stirring, over low heat until the sauce is smooth and just beginning to boil. Pour it over the chicken in the pan. Bake in preheated oven about 35 minutes, or until fork-tender, basting occasionally with sauce in the pan. Makes 6 servings.

To Freeze: Cool chicken completely. Wrap for freezing in the same baking pan in which it baked. Freeze until needed.

To Reheat: Heat oven to 425°F. Cover chicken breasts with foil. Heat 35 minutes. Remove foil and continue to heat until sauce is bubbling hot, about 10 minutes longer.

MARINATED ARTICHOKE-AND-TOMATO SALAD

1 10-ounce package frozen artichoke hearts
2 red-ripe medium-sized tomatoes
⅓ cup salad oil
3 tablespoons cider vinegar
½ teaspoon sugar
¼ teaspoon salt
Dash pepper
1 tablespoon chopped fresh dill or 1 teaspoon dried dill weed
1 teaspoon finely chopped chives
Crisp lettuce leaves

Cook artichokes as package directs. Drain well. Cut tomatoes into thin wedges. Arrange artichokes and tomatoes in a shallow pan. Combine oil, vinegar, sugar, salt, pepper, dill and chives. Pour the mixture over the vegetables. Stir gently to coat them well with the dressing. Chill at least 3 hours. Serve in lettuce cups. Makes 6 servings.

GRAHAM CRACKER MERINGUE SHELL À LA MODE

3 eggs, separated
1 cup sugar
½ cup finely chopped walnuts
1 cup graham cracker crumbs

1 teaspoon vanilla extract
½ teaspoon almond extract
1 pint vanilla or chocolate ice cream

Heat oven to 350° F. With a fork beat egg yolks until light. Blend in ½ cup of the sugar, nuts, crumbs and the extracts. Beat egg whites until soft peaks form. Gradually add remaining sugar to egg whites, continuing to beat until the meringue is very stiff. Fold the crumb mixture into the egg whites. Pour into a well-greased 9-inch pie plate, spreading out evenly. Bake in preheated oven 30 to 35 minutes or until the surface is crisp and crackled. Cut into wedges and serve warm or chilled, topped with ice cream. Makes 6 servings.

CHICKEN PAPRIKA

6 portions chicken parts, breasts or legs
¼ cup bacon drippings or vegetable oil

½ cup finely chopped onion
1 teaspoon paprika
1 teaspoon salt
¼ cup water

THE SAUCE

1 tablespoon all-purpose flour
1 teaspoon lemon juice

½ teaspoon grated lemon rind
1 cup commercial sour cream

Wipe chicken pieces with damp paper towels. Melt drippings in a heavy skillet. Add chicken and brown it lightly on all sides. Add onion and cook over medium heat until it is beginning to brown lightly. Add paprika, salt and water. Cover and simmer 30 minutes or until chicken is tender. Remove it to a heated platter. Blend together the flour, lemon juice, lemon rind and sour cream. Pour the mixture into the skillet with the chicken drippings. Heat, stirring constantly. Do not boil. Serve over chicken. Makes 6 servings.

To Freeze: Omit the sauce. Arrange cooked chicken in a shallow baking dish. Cool completely and wrap for freezing. Freeze until needed.

To Reheat: Heat oven to 425° F. Remove chicken from the freezer. Cover it with foil. Heat 35 minutes or until piping hot. Arrange chicken on a heated platter. Pour juices from the pan into a saucepan. Proceed with the sauce as above.

MOCHA PUDDING PIE

CRUST

>   *1 cup miniature marshmallows*
>   *1 4-ounce can shredded moist coconut*

Melt marshmallows in the top of a double boiler over boiling water. Stir in coconut, blending well. With buttered fingers press the mixture to the bottom and sides of an 8-inch pie plate. Chill.

FILLING

>   *1 pint coffee ice cream*
>   *1 3⅝-ounce package instant chocolate pudding mix*
>   *3 tablespoons milk*

Let ice cream soften at room temperature until it is slightly melted. In a mixing bowl blend ice cream, pudding mix and milk. Beat slowly for 1 minute or until the mixture is smooth. Pour it into the prepared crust. Chill at least 4 hours. Makes 1 8-inch pie.

BAKED SESAME CHICKEN

6 portions chicken parts,   *⅛ teaspoon pepper*
  breasts or legs   *⅓ cup melted butter or*
⅓ cup all-purpose flour   *margarine*
1 teaspoon salt   *1 tablespoon sesame seeds*

Heat oven to 400° F. Wipe chicken well with damp paper towels. In a clean paper bag combine the flour, salt and pepper. Shake chicken pieces, a few at a time, in the flour mixture, coating well. Arrange chicken in a shallow baking pan. Drizzle with melted butter. Cover the pan with foil. Bake in preheated oven 30 minutes. Remove the foil. Increase oven temperature to 450° F. Sprinkle chicken with the sesame seeds. Bake 15 minutes longer or until fork-tender and golden brown. Makes 6 servings.

To Freeze: Cool chicken completely. Wrap in the pan with freezing material. Freeze until needed.

To Reheat: Heat oven to 425° F. Remove chicken from the freezer; cover with foil; heat 30 to 35 minutes. Remove foil and continue to heat 5 to 10 minutes or until steaming hot.

RICE PILAF

⅓ cup butter or margarine   *1 6-ounce can sliced*
1 cup raw regular white   *mushrooms*
  rice   *¼ teaspoon dried orégano*
1 large onion, thinly sliced   *½ teaspoon salt*
                                  2 cups chicken broth

Melt butter in a large skillet with tight-fitting cover or in a Dutch oven. Add rice and stir it over low heat until the grains are golden brown. Add onion, undrained mushrooms, orégano, salt and chicken broth. (If more convenient, use a can of chicken broth and water to make 2 cups of liquid.) Cover and cook over low heat for 20 to 25 minutes or until the liquid is absorbed and the rice is tender. Makes 6 servings.

A SIX-RIB PORK LOIN BARGAIN

There are times every year when pork is plentiful and a fine investment. For three very different meals from the same large roast, cut two chops from a six-rib loin roast. Wrap each chop separately and freeze them, unless you plan to serve them for dinner today or tomorrow. Roast the remaining four ribs. Serve it "as is" for one meal. Freeze what is left. The menus which follow turn this leftover portion for two into tasty Pork Tetrazzini.*

Fruit Juice Cocktail
Roast Loin of Pork with Applesauce
Mashed Potatoes
Bavarian Cabbage*
Melba Toast
Canned Purple Plums
Cinnamon Toasted Pound Cake*
Tea or Coffee or Milk

Pork Tetrazzini*
Stewed Tomatoes
Cucumber Vinaigrette*
Apple and Prune Betty*
Tea or Coffee or Milk

Braised Pork Chops with Bananas and Pineapple*
Rice Pancakes*
Raw Relishes
Ice Cream   Cookies
Tea or Coffee

BAVARIAN CABBAGE

1 tablespoon bacon
  drippings or vegetable oil
2 cups finely shredded
  cabbage
½ cup boiling water
¼ teaspoon salt

Dash pepper
1 teaspoon all-purpose flour
¼ cup commercial sour
  cream
¼ teaspoon dried dill weed
  or caraway seeds

Heat bacon drippings in a medium-sized skillet. Add cabbage, boiling water, salt and pepper. Cover and cook over low heat until cabbage is tender, about 12 minutes. Remove cover. Sprinkle the flour over the cabbage. Stir and cook until the moisture is absorbed. Stir in sour cream and dill or caraway seeds. Makes 2 servings.

CINNAMON TOASTED POUND CAKE

1 slice pound cake about
  ¾ inch thick (or use 1
  individual packaged slice)

1 teaspoon soft butter or
  margarine
1 teaspoon sugar
Dash cinnamon

Just before serving, toast cake in the toaster. Spread it with butter. Sprinkle with combined sugar and cinnamon. Cut in half. Makes 2 servings.

PORK TETRAZZINI

1½ cups spaghetti broken into 1½-inch lengths
½ teaspoon instant minced onion
1 teaspoon dried parsley flakes or 1 tablespoon chopped parsley
1 3-ounce can sliced mushrooms

¾ cup canned condensed cream of mushroom soup, undiluted
¼ teaspoon Worcestershire sauce
½ cup grated Cheddar cheese
1 tablespoon chili sauce
2 cooked loin pork chops
Salt and pepper to taste

Cook spaghetti in 2 quarts of rapidly boiling salted water until tender. Drain. In the top of a double boiler combine spaghetti, onion, parsley, undrained mushrooms, soup, Worcestershire sauce, cheese and chili sauce. Cut pork from the bones and dice it in ½-inch cubes. Add pork to spaghetti mixture. Set pan over boiling water and heat 20 minutes or until steaming hot. Season to taste with salt and pepper. Makes 2 generous servings.

CUCUMBER VINAIGRETTE

1 small cucumber (about 1 cup thin slices)
2 tablespoons salad oil
1 tablespoon vinegar

1 teaspoon chopped chives
½ teaspoon chopped pimiento
Salt and pepper to taste

Peel and slice cucumber. Blend together salad oil, vinegar, chives and pimiento. Pour the mixture over the cucumber slices. Marinate in the refrigerator for about 30 minutes before serving. Season with salt and pepper. Makes 2 servings.

APPLE AND PRUNE BETTY

¾ cup ½-inch bread cubes
1 tablespoon melted butter
  or margarine
1 medium-sized apple
4 to 5 stewed, dried
  prunes, pitted
2 tablespoons brown sugar,
  packed

⅛ teaspoon ground nutmeg
Dash ground cinnamon
½ teaspoon grated lemon
  rind
2 teaspoons lemon juice
1½ tablespoons water
Light cream (optional)

Heat oven to 375° F. Stir bread cubes in the melted butter, coating them well. Peel, core and slice the apple. Sprinkle half the buttered bread cubes over the bottom of a 2-cup baking dish or individual ramekins. Cover with half the apples and prunes. Blend together the sugar, nutmeg, cinnamon and lemon rind. Sprinkle about half of this mixture over the layer of fruit. Repeat, making two layers of crumbs, fruit and sugar mixture. Drizzle with lemon juice and water. Top with remaining bread cubes. Bake in preheated oven 25 to 30 minutes or until apples are tender and crumbs lightly browned. Serve warm with cream, if desired. Makes 2 servings.

BRAISED PORK CHOPS WITH BANANAS AND PINEAPPLE

2 loin pork chops
1 teaspoon bacon drippings
  or vegetable oil
½ teaspoon salt
1 tablespoon lemon juice
½ cup water or pineapple
  juice

1 medium-ripe large banana
½ cup canned pineapple
  chunks, drained
1 tablespoon brown sugar
Dash cinnamon

In a large skillet over low heat brown chops in the drippings, turning to brown both sides. Sprinkle with salt. Drizzle with lemon juice. Add water or juice drained from pineapple chunks. Cover and simmer for 45 minutes or until chops are fork-tender, adding more water from time to time, if necessary, to keep chops from sticking. Peel the banana and slice it in 1-inch chunks. Add banana and pineapple to chops. Sprinkle the fruit with brown sugar and cinnamon. Cook over low heat until fruit is hot. Makes 2 servings.

RICE PANCAKES

2 tablespoons butter or
  margarine
½ cup cooked rice
1 egg, well beaten

Dash salt
Dash pepper
1 tablespoon milk

Heat butter in a skillet. Blend together the remaining ingredients. Fry like pancakes, using about 2 or 3 tablespoons of rice mixture for each cake. Turn to brown both sides. Makes 2 servings.

THE BONELESS SMOKED PICNIC HAM

This smoked ham in its stockinet casing will keep well, uncooked, in your refrigerator for several days, even a week. Plan to serve the Meal-in-One Boiled Dinner* menu first since the ham needs to be thoroughly cooked before using it as the featured ingredient in Orange Sweet Potatoes with Ham* or Ham Patties with Egg Sauce* which follow.

Meal-in-One Boiled Dinner*
Relish Tray of Cottage Cheese   Mustard Pickles
Celery Sticks
Whole Wheat Bread   Butter or Margarine
Canned Peach Halves
Crunchy-Topped Gingerbread*
Tea or Coffee or Milk

Orange Sweet Potatoes With Ham*
Buttered Green Vegetable
Harlequin Aspic*
Butterscotch Pudding   Cookies
Tea or Coffee

Ham Patties with Egg Sauce*
Steamed Rice
Ginger Carrots*
Coleslaw
Applesauce   Cake
Tea or Coffee or Milk

MEAL-IN-ONE BOILED DINNER

1 1¾- to 2-pound smoked
  picnic ham
6 whole peppercorns
1 bay leaf
2 teaspoons prepared horse-
  radish
2 whole cloves
2 medium-sized onions,
  peeled

2 medium-sized carrots,
  halved
2 medium-sized potatoes,
  pared and halved
2 wedges raw cabbage,
  about ⅓ of a 2-pound
  head
Salt to taste

Place ham in a Dutch oven or large kettle. Cover with water. Add peppercorns, bay leaf and horse-radish. Bring to a boil; cover; reduce heat and simmer 2 hours or until ham is almost tender. Press a clove into each onion. Add onions, carrots, potatoes and cabbage wedges. Return to boiling and simmer until vegetables are tender, about 25 minutes. Makes 2 servings with leftover ham for 2 more meals.

CRUNCHY-TOPPED GINGERBREAD

½ package gingerbread mix
1 tablespoon brown sugar
1 teaspoon flour
1 teaspoon soft butter or
  margarine

1 tablespoon broken walnut
  meats

Heat oven to 350° F. Prepare the ½ package gingerbread mix, using half of the liquid called for in the package directions. Pour batter into 4 greased custard cups. Combine the brown sugar, flour, butter and nuts. Sprinkle this mixture over the batter in 2 of the custard cups. Bake all four in preheated oven for 20 minutes or until firm to the touch. Makes 2 Crunchy-Topped Gingerbread cupcakes and 2 plain gingerbread cupcakes to save for another meal.

ORANGE SWEET POTATOES WITH HAM

*2 to 3 medium-sized
    sweet potatoes*
*4 slices boiled picnic ham,
    each about ¼ inch thick*
*3 tablespoons brown sugar,
    packed*
¼ cup orange juice
*⅛ teaspoon ground
    cinnamon*
⅛ teaspoon salt
*1 tablespoon butter or
    margarine*

Cook unpeeled sweet potatoes; cool; remove skins. Heat oven to 375° F. Grease a 1-quart casserole. Slice potatoes in half. Arrange 2 of the ham slices in the bottom of the casserole. Top with sliced sweets, then remaining ham slices. In a small saucepan combine remaining ingredients. Stir well and bring mixture to a full, rolling boil. Pour sauce over the ham and sweet potatoes. Cover and bake in preheated oven for 20 minutes. Remove cover; continue to bake 5 to 10 minutes longer or until the sauce is bubbling hot. Makes 2 servings.

HARLEQUIN ASPIC

*1 3-ounce package tomato-
    flavored salad gelatin mix*
*1 medium-sized carrot,
    shredded*
½ cup thinly sliced celery
*2 tablespoons chopped
    parsley*
Crisp lettuce leaves
*Mayonnaise or salad
    dressing*

Prepare gelatin mix as the label on the package directs. Chill until it is the consistency of unbeaten egg whites. Stir in carrot, celery and parsley. Pour into a 1-quart mold or 6 individual molds. Chill until firm. Unmold onto lettuce leaves and serve topped with mayonnaise. Makes 6 servings. Unused salad molds keep well 3 to 4 days in the refrigerator for meals later in the week.

HAM PATTIES WITH EGG SAUCE

HAM PATTIES

1 cup ground or finely
   diced cooked ham
1 tablespoon grated onion
¼ cup fine dry bread
   crumbs
1 egg, slightly beaten

1 teaspoon chopped parsley
½ teaspoon prepared
   mustard
Dash salt
2 teaspoons flour
1 tablespoon shortening

In a bowl mix ham, onion, crumbs, egg, parsley, mustard and salt. Shape mixture into 4 small patties. Dredge patties with flour, coating them on both sides. Heat shortening in a skillet and brown patties well in hot fat, turning to brown both sides. Serve with Egg Sauce. Makes 2 servings.

EGG SAUCE

½ cup canned condensed
   cream of celery soup
3 tablespoons milk

1 teaspoon capers
1 chopped hard-cooked egg
Salt and pepper to taste

In a small saucepan combine soup, milk and capers. Heat. Stir in egg. Season to taste with salt and pepper. Makes about ¾ cup sauce.

GINGER CARROTS

3 medium-sized carrots	⅛ teaspoon ground ginger
1 tablespoon butter or margarine	½ teaspoon sugar
1 teaspoon lemon juice	Salt and pepper to taste

Pare carrots and cut them into ½-inch slices. Cook in boiling salted water to cover until almost tender. Drain. Heat butter in a saucepan. Add carrots, lemon juice, ginger and sugar. Sauté, stirring frequently, for 2 to 3 minutes or until carrots are just beginning to brown. Season to taste with salt and pepper. Makes 2 servings.

THE BARGAIN LAMB PACKAGE

Perhaps no other meat bargain is geared quite as much to the family of two or the person cooking for himself or herself alone as this newcomer to the bargain list. A package of odds and ends, it contains as a rule a large lamb shank (enough meat in itself to serve two), several shoulder chops, a portion of breast suitable for roasting stuffed and/or enough lamb cut into small pieces for a pot pie or stew.

Lamb packages do vary in contents, but these menus and recipes will help you turn whatever you pull out of the bag into tasty though fantastically inexpensive meals.

For future use freeze chops, stew meat, shank and breast, all wrapped separately.

Roast Stuffed Breast of Lamb
with Brown Gravy*
Spiced Apricots
Buttered Peas   Cottage Cheese Salad
Prune Whip for Two*   Cupcake
Tea or Coffee or Milk

Baked Minted Lamb Chops*
Baked Potatoes
Mixed Vegetable Salad
Melba Toast
Individual Pineapple Upside Down Cakes*
Tea or Coffee or Milk

Braised Lamb Shank with
Spanish Rice*
Tossed Green Salad
Rye Bread   Butter or Margarine
Honey-Baked Bananas*
Tea or Coffee or Milk

Shepherd's Pie with
Mashed Potato Border*
Tomato Salad   Cottage Cheese Dressing*
Corn Muffins   Butter or Margarine
Ice Cream or Sherbet   Cookies
Tea or Coffee

ROAST STUFFED BREAST OF LAMB WITH
BROWN GRAVY

About 1½ pounds breast of lamb²
Salt and pepper
2 tablespoons butter or margarine
1 small onion, finely chopped
¼ cup hot water
2 tablespoons chopped parsley or 2 teaspoons dry parsley flakes
1 cup packaged stuffing mix
2 canned spiced apricots
Parsley sprigs

Heat oven to 350° F. Wipe lamb with damp paper towels. Trim off excess fat. Cut a pocket between the layer of meat and the rib bones. Sprinkle the inside of the pocket with salt and pepper. In a saucepan melt butter. Add onion, hot water, chopped parsley and stuffing mix. Blend and use as stuffing for the pocket in the lamb. Insert small skewers across the opening. Using heavy cord, lace the pocket closed. Roast in preheated oven for 1¼ hours or until well browned. Remove the roast to a heated platter. Garnish with spiced apricots and parsley. Makes 2 servings.

² 1½ pounds may seem like much too much lamb for 2. But this cut of lamb, like spareribs, includes rib bones. In spite of the 1½ pounds called for, breast of lamb is so inexpensive that it is a rare bargain.

BROWN GRAVY

Measure 2 tablespoons drippings from the pan into a small saucepan. Stir in 1 tablespoon flour, ¼ teaspoon salt and a dash of pepper. Stir over medium heat until the flour is well browned. Gradually stir in ¾ cup water or chicken broth. Cook and stir until gravy is smooth and thickened. Serve with the lamb. Makes about ¾ cup.

PRUNE WHIP FOR TWO

8 to 10 stewed prunes,
  pitted
2 egg whites
¼ cup sugar

¼ teaspoon cinnamon
¼ teaspoon grated lemon
  rind
Dash salt

Cut prunes into small bits and mash them well. Beat the egg whites stiff. Gradually beat in the sugar, continuing to beat until the egg whites stand in stiff peaks when the beater is raised. Fold in the prunes, cinnamon, lemon rind and salt. Makes 2 servings.

BAKED MINTED LAMB CHOPS

2 shoulder lamb chops
Salt and pepper
2 tablespoons fresh mint
  leaves or 2 teaspoons
  dried mint leaves
2 tablespoons sugar

1 tablespoon vinegar
⅓ cup water
½ teaspoon grated lemon
  rind
Dash salt

Heat oven to 350° F. Arrange chops in a shallow baking dish or 9-inch pie plate. Sprinkle them with salt and pepper. In a small saucepan combine mint leaves, sugar, vinegar, water, lemon rind and salt. Bring the mixture to a boil. Cook until reduced about half in volume. Pour mint mixture over the chops. Bake in preheated oven for 45 minutes or until tender and well browned. Makes 2 servings.

INDIVIDUAL PINEAPPLE UPSIDE DOWN CAKES

2 tablespoons butter or
  margarine
4 tablespoons light brown
  sugar, packed
¼ cup sifted cake flour
¼ teaspoon baking powder
Dash salt
1 egg, separated

1 tablespoon melted butter
¼ teaspoon almond extract
2 tablespoons sugar
2 well-drained canned
  pineapple slices
2 maraschino cherries
Light cream (optional)

Heat oven to 350° F. Measure 1 tablespoon of the butter
and 2 tablespoons brown sugar into each of 2 custard cups.
Place the cups in a 9-inch plate or on a cookie sheet, and set
them in the oven. Butter and brown sugar will melt while you
prepare the batter.

Sift together flour, baking powder and salt. Beat the egg
yolk well. Stir in melted butter and almond extract. Beat the
egg white until soft peaks form. Gradually beat in the sugar,
continuing to beat until the egg white is stiff and glossy.
Blend together flour and egg yolk mixtures. Fold in the egg
white.

Remove custard cups from the oven. Arrange a pineapple
slice and maraschino cherry over the melted brown sugar.
Spread the batter over the pineapple slices. Bake 25 to 30
minutes or until lightly browned and firm to the touch. Serve
warm or chilled, with cream if desired. Makes 2 servings.

BRAISED LAMB SHANK WITH
SPANISH RICE

1 large lamb shank
1 bay leaf
3 whole cloves
1 teaspoon salt
Boiling water
1 cup tomato juice
½ cup water

½ cup raw regular white rice
1 small onion, thinly sliced
¼ cup fresh or frozen diced green pepper
½ teaspoon salt
⅛ teaspoon pepper

In a Dutch oven or heavy kettle with tight-fitting cover brown the lamb shank slowly, turning to brown it well on all sides. Add the bay leaf, cloves, the 1 teaspoon salt and enough boiling water to cover. Bring to a boil. Cover the kettle; reduce heat and simmer for 1¼ hours or until the meat is very tender. Drain off and discard the liquid and fat.

In the same Dutch oven combine lamb shank, the tomato juice and water. Bring to a boil. Stir in rice, onion, green pepper, salt and pepper. Cover; turn heat to medium and cook 20 to 25 minutes or until liquid is absorbed and rice tender and fluffy. Makes 2 servings.

HONEY-BAKED BANANAS

2 small firm bananas
2 tablespoons honey
1 tablespoon ready-to-eat cereal crumbs (crushed corn or rice flakes)

1 tablespoon flaked coconut (optional)
1 teaspoon butter or margarine
Dash cinnamon

Heat oven to 425° F. Peel bananas and place them on a square of foil. Crimp the edges of the foil around the sides of the bananas to hold in the juices. Drizzle bananas with honey. Sprinkle with cereal crumbs and coconut, if desired. Dot with butter. Sprinkle with cinnamon. Bake in preheated oven 8 to 10 minutes or until bananas are lightly browned and very tender. Makes 2 servings.

SHEPHERD'S PIE WITH MASHED POTATO BORDER

½ pound boneless lamb, cut in 1-inch pieces (about 1½ cups)
2 teaspoons vegetable oil or shortening
1 tablespoon minced onion
1 tablespoon flour
Dash pepper
½ teaspoon salt
1 cup boiling water
1 bay leaf (optional)
2 carrots, scraped and diced
2 to 3 green onions, thinly sliced, tops and all
Instant whipped potatoes
1 teaspoon melted butter or margarine

Remove any gristle from lamb. Heat oil in a skillet. Add onion and cook 1 to 2 minutes. Combine flour, pepper and salt in a pie plate and roll the lamb in the flour mixture, coating it well. Brown lamb in hot fat in the skillet, turning to brown all sides. Add boiling water and bay leaf. Cover and simmer for 1 hour. Add carrots and green onions. Cover again and continue to cook until vegetables are tender—10 to 12 minutes. Remove bay leaf. Pour meat and vegetables into a greased 3- or 4-cup casserole. Heat oven to 425 F. Prepare instant whipped potatoes as package directs for 2 servings. Spoon them in a border around the edge of the casserole. Drizzle with melted butter and bake in preheated oven for 7 to 10 minutes, or until potato border is beginning to brown lightly. Makes 2 servings.

COTTAGE CHEESE DRESSING

¼ cup cottage cheese
¼ cup bottled French dressing
2 pimiento-stuffed olives, chopped

Blend the ingredients in a small jar and chill until used. Makes about ⅓ cup or enough for two salads. Use within 3 days.

Chapter Four

COOKING FOR ONE

The saying "Two can live as cheaply as one" has been making the rounds for too many years. It may have caused you some concern if you are retiring as a family of one. Cheer up! There's little truth in such a quotation. Maybe the same rent can house two people as cheaply as one, but that's about as far as any saving goes. One person living alone can enjoy tempting, tasty meals for many dollars a month less than it would cost to prepare the same meals for a twosome. No matter whether meals are for a dozen or for one alone, it's waste that is the villain always ready to make you spend more than you had anticipated. Those tiny odds and ends thrown away as too infinitesimal to bother saving do make a difference. In Chapter Two under the heading of Freezing Bits of This and That many of these penny-savers were discussed, but it doesn't hurt to review some of them here.

• *A small onion.* You probably will need only about one third of that onion for the casserole dish to serve one which you are preparing. If the rest of the onion seems hardly worth saving, remind yourself that one onion is enough for three casseroles. So why use three onions for them? Chop what you don't need now, wrap it for freezing, and pop it into the freezer. Even in the refrigerator, well wrapped, it will keep for several days. Then the next time you need onion, there will be no peeling, no chopping for you to do.

• The same is true of *green pepper,* a piece of *carrot* or a *stalk of celery.* And every penny saved goes into that growing kitty for extras.

• See what Chapter Two says about dabs of *whipped*

cream and *one lone egg white* too. It is wasted dabs of just such foods that give the impression that two can live as cheaply as one.

· Even that *half slice of buttered toast* you couldn't finish at breakfast time can be a penny in the bank for future use. Haven't you, dozens of times, toasted a fresh slice of bread for crumbs—a whole slice when you needed only a tablespoonful? Dry out that leftover half slice thoroughly. Crumble it and store in a small, well-sealed jar.

With these few common "leaks" in the food budget to start you sleuthing, you can go on to other detective work and ferret out other villains that break the food budget. Every time you eliminate a culprit, there go more pennies into the old teapot for that special something you thought you couldn't afford.

Cooking for one isn't much different from cooking for two or more. In fact, many of the recipes for main dishes that can be made to eat-part-now—freeze-the-rest-to-eat-later found in Chapter Three are just as valid for the family of one as for anyone else. You will buy with an eye on the weekend specials just like everyone else too. Even though your freezer space may be the smallest possible, it can be relied upon to save you money, time and effort. It helps make meals varied and enjoyable.

It isn't the breakfasts or lunches that are a problem when cooking for one. Eggs, fruits, juices, cereals, sandwiches, soups—all make these meals simple to prepare for anyone. You will find dinners will be easier to shop for and less expensive if you plan three meals from the same cut of meat. Once the main meat dish is settled, small cans of vegetables, ice cream, canned or fresh fruits, individually packaged cupcakes, etc., give ready variety for the rest of the meal without waste from leftovers. If you have been cooking for a large family most of your life, the following menus and recipes for one will help you adjust your thinking and planning. And if you have been a hurried, harried business executive with very little time or energy for many cooking sprees, these are for you too. Now is your chance to cultivate your culinary talents and astonish your friends with the good meals you seem to pull out of a hat. With time now for creative hobbies, you'll find cooking for yourself and occasionally for your friends a hobby that becomes more exciting with each success. With time now to relax at mealtime, time to enjoy those heady aromas, don't be surprised if some favorite foods which may have been placed on the forbidden list agree with you again better than they ever did.

WHEN LAMB STEW IS BARGAIN PRICED

Boneless lamb for stew, about 1¼ to 1½ pounds of it, gives you the meat for these three lamb main dishes.

Fruit Juice Cocktail
Savory Lamb Stew with Vegetables*
Assorted Relishes (Cherry Tomatoes, Olives, Mixed Pickles)
Parker House Roll Butter or Margarine
Ice Cream with Make-Ahead Melba Sauce*
Tea or Coffee

Lamb Curry with Fluffy Rice*
Toasted Coconut Chutney Roasted Peanuts
Cottage Cheese and Tomato Salad
Heated Packaged Muffin Butter or Margarine
Baked Apple
Tea or Coffee or Milk

Lamb Stew with Noodles*
Dutch Spinach*
Tossed Green Salad
Fruit Whip for One*
Tea or Coffee or Milk

FROZEN LAMB IN STOCK

This recipe for 4 servings of Frozen Lamb in Stock gives you in one cooking session the cooked, ready-to-use lamb which turns into stew for today, a delectable lamb curry all ready for the finishing touches, and enough lamb stew to serve with noodles for another meal.

3 tablespoons all-purpose flour
1 teaspoon salt
⅛ teaspoon pepper
1¼ to 1½ pounds trimmed boneless lamb, cut into 1-inch cubes

2 tablespoons bacon drippings or vegetable oil
2½ cups water
1 small bay leaf

Blend flour, salt and pepper in a pie plate. Dredge meat in the flour mixture, coating all pieces well. Heat the drippings in a skillet; add lamb and cook, turning frequently to brown all sides. Add water and bay leaf. Cover; simmer until tender, about 1¼ hours, adding a little more water from time to time, if necessary, to keep liquid bubbling in the pan. Put ¼ of the meat and stock in each of 4 freezer containers. Seal; freeze until needed to prepare Savory Lamb Stew with Vegetables,* Lamb Curry* and Lamb Stew with Noodles.* You will have completed the longest part of the cooking period for all three recipes.

SAVORY LAMB STEW WITH VEGETABLES

1 container Frozen Lamb in
Stock*
1 cup water
1 medium-sized carrot,
scraped and sliced
1 small potato, pared and
cut in half
1 small onion, peeled and
sliced

Dash powdered thyme
(optional)
⅛ teaspoon salt
Dash pepper
1 teaspoon chopped parsley
Few celery leaves
(optional)
¼ cup frozen peas

Remove any excess fat from lamb. Bring water to a boil
in a saucepan with tight-fitting cover. Add all ingredients
except peas. Bring mixture to a boil; reduce heat; cover and
simmer until meat is thawed and vegetables about half done.
Add more water, if necessary, to keep the liquid bubbling
in the pan around the meat and vegetables. Add peas and
continue to cook until vegetables are tender. Turn heat high.
Reduce liquid to about ⅓ cup. Makes 1 generous serving.

MAKE-AHEAD MELBA SAUCE

1 10-ounce package frozen
raspberries, thawed
½ cup currant jelly

1½ teaspoons cornstarch
1 tablespoon cold water

Combine berries and jelly in a saucepan. Bring to a boil.
Blend the cornstarch and water to a smooth paste and stir
it into the berries. Cook, stirring, until the sauce is clear and
thickened. Strain through a coarse sieve. Keep in a covered
jar in the refrigerator. Makes about 1 cup sauce to use as a
topping for canned fruits or ice cream.

LAMB CURRY WITH FLUFFY RICE

2 packages Frozen Lamb in
Stock*
1 cup water
1 tablespoon butter or
margarine
1 tablespoon chopped onion
½ cup canned applesauce
1 tablespoon all-purpose
flour

1 teaspoon curry powder[1]
Dash allspice
1½ cups hot cooked rice
Bottled chutney (optional)
Toasted coconut (optional)
Roasted peanuts (optional)

Remove excess fat from frozen lamb. Empty lamb into a heavy saucepan with a tight-fitting cover. Add the water. Cover and heat slowly until the lamb is thawed and the gravy beginning to boil. Meanwhile, heat the butter in a small skillet. Add the onion and cook, stirring occasionally, until the onion is lightly browned. Stir in applesauce. Blend together the flour, curry powder and allspice; stir into the onion mixture. Stir the flour mixture into the lamb and cook, stirring constantly, until the gravy is thickened. Serve on fluffy rice topped, if desired, with chutney, coconut and roasted peanuts. Makes 2 servings. If preparing dinner for yourself alone, cool half of the lamb thoroughly. Freeze in an airtight freezer container for another meal.

[1] If you like your curries strong, add more curry powder to taste.

LAMB STEW WITH NOODLES

*1 package Frozen Lamb
in Stock**
½ cup water
*2 tablespoons frozen or
fresh chopped green
pepper*

1 tablespoon chopped onion
1½ cups packaged noodles
1 teaspoon chopped parsley

Remove any excess fat from lamb. In a medium-sized saucepan combine lamb chunks in their gravy, water, green pepper and onion. Cover and cook over low heat until meat is steaming hot and vegetables tender. Cook noodles in boiling salted water as the package label directs. Drain them well. Stir the noodles into the lamb mixture. Sprinkle with parsley. Makes 1 generous serving.

DUTCH SPINACH

*½ of a 10-ounce package
frozen chopped spinach*
½ cup boiling water
Dash salt
*2 teaspoons butter or
margarine*

1 teaspoon flour
Dash nutmeg
*Dash powdered garlic
(optional)*
Lemon wedge

In a saucepan combine spinach, water and salt. Bring to a boil; reduce heat and simmer for 4 to 5 minutes or until spinach is done. Drain *well*. In the saucepan in which the spinach cooked, melt the butter. Blend in flour, nutmeg and, if desired, powdered garlic. Cook over low heat, stirring constantly until the flour is golden brown. Remove from heat; add spinach and toss to blend with browned flour. Serve with a wedge of lemon. Makes 1 serving.

FRUIT WHIP FOR ONE

1 canned peach half or 4 stewed prunes	⅛ teaspoon cinnamon
1 egg white	¼ teaspoon grated lemon rind
2 tablespoons sugar	

Mash peach half, or pit prunes and cut them into bits. Beat the egg white stiff. Gradually beat in the sugar, continuing to beat until the egg white is very stiff. Fold in the fruit, cinnamon and lemon rind. Makes 1 serving.

CUBED LEAN VEAL

Most frequently cubed veal comes in two individual portions per package and makes a good no-waste purchase for anyone, especially for the family of one. Pressed deceptively thin and flat in the cubing process, they may look too huge to serve one, but their average weight is 4 to 4½ ounces each.

Veal Scallopini*
Creamed Small Potatoes
Asparagus Salad
Melba Toast
Ginger-Honey Baked Pears*
Tea or Coffee or Milk

Veal Paprika*
Buttered Hominy Grits or
Parsley Potato
Buttered Green Vegetable
Minted Frozen Pineapple Chunks*   Cookies
Tea or Coffee or Milk

Chilled Apple Juice
Veal Cutlet in Tomato Sauce*
Baked Potato
Buttered Spinach with Lemon Wedge
Individual Mocha Icebox Cakes*
Tea or Coffee or Milk

VEAL SCALLOPINI

1 veal scallop, about 4 ounces	*Salt and pepper*
	¼ teaspoon grated lemon rind
1 teaspoon flour	
2 teaspoons olive or vegetable oil	*2 teaspoons lemon juice*
	2 tablespoons water
1 teaspoon butter or margarine	*1 teaspoon capers*

Dust the veal on both sides with flour. Heat oil and butter in a small skillet. Add veal; sprinkle with salt and pepper, and cook over low heat until nicely browned on both sides. Sprinkle with lemon rind and lemon juice. Add water. Cover tightly and cook over low heat until all moisture has evaporated and veal is tender. Serve with a sprinkling of capers. Makes 1 serving.

GINGER-HONEY BAKED PEARS

2 medium-sized firm, ripe   3 tablespoons finely
  pears   chopped candied ginger
¼ cup honey   3 tablespoons water

Heat oven to 350° F. Wash and peel pears. Cut them into halves lengthwise and remove cores. Arrange them, rounded sides down, in a 1-quart baking dish. Pour honey over the pears and sprinkle them with the candied ginger. Pour the water into the pan around the pears. Cover and bake 30 minutes. Remove the cover, baste with the liquid in the pan and continue to bake, uncovered, until pears are fork-tender and slightly glazed. Serve warm or chilled. Makes 2 to 3 servings. Keep any left from your dinner in a small covered dish in the refrigerator for lunch or dinner another day. Pears will keep refrigerated for 4 to 5 days.

VEAL PAPRIKA

1 scallop of veal, about 4   Dash pepper
  ounces   ¾ teaspoon paprika
1 teaspoon bacon drippings   ½ cup boiling water
  or vegetable oil   ¾ teaspoon flour
1 tablespoon chopped onion   1 tablespoon cold water
Dash garlic salt   3 tablespoons commercial
⅛ teaspoon salt   sour cream

In a small skillet sauté veal in hot bacon drippings, turning to brown both sides well. Add onion; sprinkle with garlic salt, salt and pepper and paprika. Add boiling water. Cover and simmer 20 to 25 minutes or until veal is fork-tender, adding a little more water from time to time, if necessary, to keep veal from sticking. Remove veal to your serving plate and keep warm. Stir flour into pan drippings. Slowly stir in cold water and sour cream. Heat, but do not boil. Pour sauce over veal. Makes 1 serving.

MINTED FROZEN PINEAPPLE CHUNKS

¼ cup apple-mint jelly
3 tablespoons water
1 13¼-ounce can frozen pineapple chunks, partly defrosted

In a small saucepan combine the jelly and water. Bring to a boil. Cook 3 minutes or until the syrup is smooth and the consistency of corn syrup. Empty pineapple into a bowl. Pour mint syrup over. Chill at least 1 hour. Makes 2 to 3 servings.

VEAL CUTLET IN TOMATO SAUCE

The menu which includes Veal Cutlet in Tomato Sauce suggests a baked potato. So time the veal cutlet to go into the same oven with the potato the last 10 minutes of baking time. Or, if you are not serving a baked potato, preheat the oven to 400° F. and bake the cutlet 10 minutes as directed below.

1 veal scallop, about 4 ounces
2 teaspoons flour
1 tablespoon olive or vegetable oil
Salt and pepper
1 small onion, thinly sliced

1 tablespoon chopped green pepper (optional)
½ cup canned tomato sauce
¼ cup water
⅛ teaspoon orégano
1 thin slice Mozzarella cheese

Dredge veal in flour, coating both sides well. Heat oil in a small skillet. Brown veal in hot oil, turning to brown both sides. Sprinkle with salt and pepper. Add onion and green pepper, if desired. Cook until onion is beginning to brown. Add tomato sauce, water and orégano. Cover and simmer for 10 minutes. Arrange veal and the tomato sauce in a small, shallow baking pan or pie plate. Top with the cheese. Bake in preheated oven 10 minutes or until cheese is melted. Makes 1 serving.

INDIVIDUAL MOCHA ICEBOX CAKES

½ cup heavy cream
½ teaspoon instant coffee powder

¼ teaspoon vanilla extract
16 crisp, round chocolate cookies

Whip cream. Stir in powdered coffee and vanilla extract. Spread the cookies with whipped cream. Stack, making 4 sets each 4 cookies high. Press each set of cookies together gently. Arrange them in a shallow pan. Refrigerate 4 hours before serving. Or refrigerate 4 hours; then freeze, unwrapped, just until the whipped cream is firm. Then wrap each individual icebox cake in freezer material and freeze until needed. Makes 4 servings.

CHICKEN—THE YEAR-ROUND BARGAIN

Here are three different as can be meals from one three-pound frying chicken.

Chicken with Orange Sauce*
Fluffy Rice
Buttered Broccoli
Tomato Salad
Roll or Melba Toast Butter or Margarine
Canned Kadota Figs in Cream
Tea or Coffee or Milk

Small Glass of Grapefruit Juice
Chicken Divan*
Tossed Salad
Packaged Corn Muffin Butter or Margarine
Fruit Sherbet Cookie
Tea or Coffee or Milk

Chicken Tetrazzini*
Buttered Asparagus
Fruit Salad
Melba Toast or Crackers
Spiced Orange and Grapefruit Cup*
Tea or Coffee

CHICKEN WITH ORANGE SAUCE

*½ split breast of chicken or
  1 drumstick and 1 thigh
1 tablespoon flour
¼ teaspoon salt
Dash pepper*

*2 teaspoons shortening or
  vegetable oil
2 tablespoons frozen orange
  juice concentrate
½ cup water
Dash of nutmeg*

Wash chicken and dry it well with a paper towel. Combine flour, salt and pepper in a pie plate. Roll chicken in the flour mixture, coating it well. Heat shortening in a small skillet. Brown chicken in hot fat, turning to brown all sides. Add the orange juice concentrate and water. (Or use ⅔ cup fresh or canned orange juice.) Cover and cook over very low heat for 25 to 30 minutes or until chicken is tender. Peek occasionally and add a bit more water, if necessary, to keep juice simmering around the chicken. Add a dash of nutmeg. Makes 1 serving.

Boil the remaining chicken. When tender, pick the meat from the bones and divide it in half. Wrap and freeze each half separately. Use half for Chicken Divan* and the rest for Chicken Tetrazzini.*

CHICKEN DIVAN

*About ½ of a 10-ounce
  package frozen broccoli
Frozen chicken (the half
  left from Chicken with
  Orange Sauce*),
  defrosted*

*½ cup undiluted cream of
  chicken soup
1 tablespoon grated
  Parmesan cheese*

Heat oven to 350° F. Cook broccoli in boiling salted water as label on package directs. Drain well. Grease an

8-inch pie plate. Arrange broccoli over the bottom of the pan. Top it with chicken and pour the soup over. Sprinkle with the cheese and bake in preheated oven for 30 minutes or until lightly browned and bubbling hot. Makes 1 serving.

CHICKEN TETRAZZINI

1 cup spaghetti broken in 1-inch lengths

Frozen chicken (the half left from Chicken with Orange Sauce*), defrosted

½ cup undiluted cream of chicken soup

¼ cup milk

½ teaspoon instant minced onion

⅓ cup grated Cheddar cheese

1 teaspoon parsley flakes or 1 tablespoon chopped parsley

½ teaspoon Worcestershire sauce

Cook spaghetti in 3 cups of boiling water. Drain. Dice chicken. Combine cooked spaghetti, chicken and remaining ingredients in the top of a double boiler. Set boiler top in place over boiling water and cook for 20 minutes, or until cheese is melted and mixture steaming hot. Makes 1 serving.

SPICED ORANGE AND GRAPEFRUIT CUP

1 seedless orange, peeled and sectioned

1 grapefruit, peeled and sectioned

3 tablespoons sugar

½ cup water

Small stick cinnamon

3 whole cloves

1 tablespoon sliced candied ginger (optional)

Combine fruit sections in a small bowl. Squeeze out any juice remaining around the connective tissue of the orange and grapefruit and add the juice to the fruit in the bowl. In a small saucepan combine sugar, water and spices. Bring mixture to a boil; reduce heat and simmer about 3 minutes or until liquid is reduced to about ¼ cup. Cool; remove cinnamon stick and cloves; pour over fruit and chill. Makes 2 servings.

THREE MEALS FROM A POUND OF ROUND STEAK

For these three menus buy one pound of round steak cut 1 inch thick. Divide it in thirds—one third to use when preparing each menu. Wrap and freeze the two portions not needed today. Defrost about ½ hour before using in other recipes.

Swiss Steak*
Paprika Buttered Potatoes
Canned or Frozen Wax Beans
Tossed Green Salad
Packaged Date-Nut Bread Cream Cheese and Jelly
Glass of Milk
Tea or Coffee

Beef Stew with Noodles for One*
Buttered Carrots
Lettuce and Tomato Salad
Roll or Melba Toast Butter or Margarine
Frozen Melon Balls in Grape Juice
Tea or Coffee or Milk

Hot Tomato Juice
Individual Beef and Vegetable Pie
with Fluffy Rice Border*
Crisp Green Salad
Toasted English Muffin   Butter or Margarine
Applesauce   Gingersnaps
Tea or Coffee or Milk

SWISS STEAK

*⅓ pound round steak cut
  1 inch thick
2 teaspoons flour
¼ teaspoon salt
Dash pepper*

*2 teaspoons vegetable oil or
  shortening
1 cup tomato juice
1 small onion, peeled and
  sliced*

Lay meat on a breadboard. Sprinkle it with half of the
flour and the salt and pepper. Pound in the flour using the
rim of a sturdy saucer or a meat pounder. Turn meat and
pound the rest of the flour into the other side. Heat the oil
in a skillet with a tight-fitting cover. Brown meat well on
both sides. Turn heat low and add tomato juice and onion.
Cover and simmer for 1 hour, adding a little water from time
to time if necessary, to keep meat from sticking. Makes 1
serving.

BEEF STEW WITH NOODLES FOR ONE

*⅓ pound round steak
2 teaspoons flour
¼ teaspoon salt
Dash pepper
2 teaspoons vegetable oil*

*1 bay leaf
1 teaspoon instant minced
  onion
1½ cups water
1 cup packaged noodles*

Cut beef into 1-inch cubes. Combine flour, salt and pepper. Roll beef in the flour mixture, coating it well. Heat oil in a heavy saucepan with tight-fitting cover. Brown beef well on all sides in oil. Add the bay leaf, onion and water. Cover and simmer for 1 hour or until meat is very tender. Sprinkle in the noodles, adding a little more water, if necessary, to keep liquid boiling around the noodles. Cover and cook for about 8 minutes or until noodles are done. Makes 1 hearty serving.

INDIVIDUAL BEEF AND VEGETABLE PIE WITH FLUFFY RICE BORDER

⅓ pound round steak
2 teaspoons flour
¼ teaspoon salt
Dash pepper
2 teaspoons salad oil
1½ cups water

1 medium onion, peeled
  and sliced
1 carrot, scraped and cut
  in half
⅓ cup raw regular white
  rice

Cut beef in 1-inch cubes. Combine flour, salt and pepper. Roll beef in flour mixture, coating it well. Heat the oil in a heavy saucepan with tight-fitting cover. Brown meat in oil, turning to brown all sides. Add the 1½ cups water. Bring to a boil. Cover the pan and simmer for 45 minutes. Add the onion and carrot and cook until tender, about 20 minutes, adding a bit more water to the pan, if necessary, to keep the beef and vegetables from sticking. Meanwhile, cook the rice, following the directions on the package label. Serve beef and vegetables in a ramekin bordered with rice. Makes 1 serving.

BONUS MEALS FROM A PORK ROAST

One five-rib pork roast makes the three main dishes for these tasty meals. Have your butcher cut off two ribs as one thick chop. Then have him cut a pocket in the chop for stuffing (for Baked Stuffed Pork Chop*). Roast the remaining three ribs. Serve once as roast pork and use the leftover roast to make Sweet and Sour Pork* for another meal.

Roast Pork   Cream Gravy
Pickled Crab Apples
Baked Sweet Potatoes
Stewed Tomatoes
Buttered Roll or Melba Toast
Tapioca Cream with Strawberry Jam*
Tea or Coffee or Milk

Sweet and Sour Pork*
Steamed Rice
Lettuce Salad   Russian Dressing
Buttered Roll
Packaged Almond Cookies
Tea

Cup of Cream of Celery Soup
Baked Stuffed Pork Chop*
Mashed Turnips
Cabbage, Pear and Raisin Slaw*
Heated Roll   Butter or Margarine
Mixed Fruit Compote
Tea or Coffee or Milk

TAPIOCA CREAM WITH STRAWBERRY JAM

1 egg, separated
1 cup milk
2½ tablespoons sugar
Dash salt

1½ tablespoons quick-
cooking tapioca
¼ teaspoon vanilla extract
1 teaspoon strawberry jam

In a saucepan combine the egg yolk and ½ cup of the milk. Stir in the remaining milk, 1½ tablespoons of the sugar, salt and tapioca. Cook over medium heat until the mixture comes to a boil, stirring constantly. (Do not overcook. The mixture thickens as it cools.) Remove from heat. Beat egg white until soft peaks form. Gradually beat in remaining tablespoon of sugar, continuing to beat until the egg white is very stiff. Fold the hot tapioca and vanilla into the egg white, blending well. Cool. Stir once after 15 minutes. Chill. Serve topped with jam. Makes 2 servings—one for dinner, one for a bedtime snack or for lunch tomorrow.

SWEET AND SOUR PORK

Leftover pork roast (about
half of your 3-rib roast)
1 teaspoon shortening
1 slice canned pineapple
⅔ cup pineapple juice
1 small onion, thinly sliced,
or 1 scallion cut in
1-inch lengths

Dash salt
1 teaspoon vinegar
1 tablespoon brown sugar
⅛ teaspoon ground ginger
1 teaspoon soy sauce
½ teaspoon cornstarch

Dice pork. Brown it in a small saucepan in hot shortening. Cut the pineapple into 6 to 8 pieces. Add pineapple, pineapple juice, onion slices, salt and vinegar. Cover the pan and simmer for 5 minutes. Meanwhile blend together the remaining ingredients. Stir the cornstarch mixture into the pork, stirring constantly until the sauce is clear and slightly thickened. Serve with rice. Makes 1 serving.

BAKED STUFFED PORK CHOP

1 double pork chop, with a
  pocket for stuffing
Salt
¼ cup coarsely crumbled
  saltine cracker crumbs

½ teaspoon parsley flakes
¼ teaspoon instant minced
  onion
1 3-ounce can sliced
  mushrooms

Heat oven to 350° F. Sprinkle the inside of the pocket in the chop with salt. Combine the cracker crumbs, parsley flakes and onion. Drain mushrooms, saving juice. Add the mushrooms to the crumb mixture and toss with a fork to blend the stuffing. Spoon stuffing into the pocket in the chop. Place stuffed chop in a 1-quart casserole or a small baking dish with a cover. Pour the drained mushroom liquid around the chop. Cover and bake in preheated oven for 1 hour. Uncover and continue to bake for 10 to 15 minutes, or until chop is well browned and tender. Makes 1 generous serving.

CABBAGE, PEAR AND RAISIN SLAW

1 canned pear half, well
  drained
½ cup finely shredded
  green cabbage
1 tablespoon seedless raisins
½ teaspoon lemon juice

½ teaspoon sugar
⅛ teaspoon anise or fennel
  seeds (optional)
2 tablespoons mayonnaise
Salt to taste

Dice pear. In a small bowl combine pear, cabbage and raisins. Blend together lemon juice, sugar, anise seeds and mayonnaise. Stir dressing into cabbage mixture, tossing lightly with a fork to coat all ingredients well. Season to taste with salt. For a subtle blending of flavors, chill at least 30 minutes before serving. Makes 1 serving.

NO-WASTE SHRIMP MEALS

Prepare two different one-serving recipes from one pound of fresh shrimp. Or use a seven-ounce package of frozen ready-to-cook shrimp. Or double a recipe and serve as a company dinner entree to yourself and one other.

Fresh Fruit Cup
Stirred Shrimp*
Parsley Rice
Broiled Tomato Halves*
Lemon Sponge Pudding*
Tea or Coffee

Shrimp and Rice Creole for One*
Buttered Broccoli
Celery Hearts   Carrot Sticks
Whole Wheat Bread   Butter or Margarine
Greengage Plums
Tea or Coffee or Milk

STIRRED SHRIMP

2 teaspoons butter or
margarine
½ pound raw shrimp,
shelled and deveined, or
½ of a 7-ounce package
frozen ready-to-cook shrimp

¾ teaspoon cornstarch
⅛ teaspoon salt
1 tablespoon sherry
2 teaspoons chopped chives
Dash ground ginger

In a small skillet melt butter. Combine shrimp and remaining ingredients in a bowl and stir them to mix well. Cook shrimp mixture in hot butter over low heat, stirring frequently with a fork until shrimp is pink and tender—about 4 to 5 minutes, depending upon the size of the shrimp. Makes 1 generous serving.

BROILED TOMATO HALVES

1 small ripe tomato
Salt and pepper
1 teaspoon chopped chives

1 teaspoon melted butter or
margarine
1 teaspoon Parmesan cheese

Heat broiler. Cut tomato in half crosswise. Make ⅛-inch-deep slashes about ½ inch apart over the cut surfaces. Sprinkle with salt, pepper and chives. Drizzle with melted butter and sprinkle with Parmesan cheese. Broil about 5 inches from the source of heat for 5 minutes or until cheese begins to brown. Makes 1 serving.

LEMON SPONGE PUDDING

⅓ cup sugar
2 teaspoons butter or
   margarine
1 teaspoon grated lemon
   rind

1 egg, separated
1½ tablespoons flour
3 tablespoons lemon juice
½ cup milk
Dash salt

Heat oven to 350° F. Cream together the sugar, butter and lemon rind. Add the egg yolk to the sugar mixture and beat well. Stir in flour, lemon juice, milk and salt. Beat the egg white stiff. Fold it into the yolk mixture. Pour into 2 well-greased custard cups (¾-cup capacity). Set custard cups in a shallow baking dish or pie plate filled with 1 inch of hot water. Bake in preheated oven for 30 minutes. Serve warm or chilled. Makes 2 servings.

SHRIMP AND RICE CREOLE FOR ONE

½ pound raw shrimp,
   shelled and deveined,
   or ½ of a 7-ounce
   package frozen ready-to-
   cook shrimp
1 cup boiling water
Dash salt
1 slice lemon

¾ cup cooked rice
½ cup canned tomatoes
1 teaspoon instant minced
   onion
Dash powdered thyme
2 to 3 pimiento-stuffed
   olives, thinly sliced
Salt and pepper to taste

In a saucepan combine shrimp, boiling water, salt and lemon slice. Bring to a boil; cover and cook 5 minutes or until shrimp is pink and tender. Drain well. Discard lemon slice. Combine shrimp and remaining ingredients in the top of a double boiler over boiling water. Heat. Makes 1 generous main-dish serving.

FOR A COZY TEA PARTY FOR TWO,
THREE, OR MORE

If you are like everyone else who lives alone, there is many an afternoon when you say to yourself, "If only I had something to serve, I'd call So-and-So over for a cup of tea and catch up on the news." So here's the menu to let you reach for the telephone knowing you have the makings for a perfect tea party. Festive Petits Fours,* made for less than 2 cents apiece, can be made days ahead of time and kept in the freezer until you happen to feel like serving them. Make more as you use them up to keep on hand for other spur-of-the-moment gab-fests.

Spur-of-the-Moment Tea Party

Festive Petits Fours*
Cinnamon Toast (optional)
Steaming Hot Tea with Lemon Slices

FESTIVE PETITS FOURS*

1 slice individually packaged pound cake
¼ cup sifted confectioners' sugar
Milk
Few drops lemon or almond extract
2 walnut or pecan halves, chopped
1 maraschino cherry, cut in 8 strips

Cut pound cake slice in half lengthwise, then in quarters crosswise, making 8 tiny cake squares. Arrange them in a pie plate and freeze about 1 hour or until firm enough so that crumbs will not blend into the icing when you frost them. Blend together confectioners' sugar and enough milk to make a thin frosting about the consistency of thin custard sauce. Stir in extract. Stick a toothpick into a frozen cake square. Holding the toothpick, dip the cake into the frosting; remove the toothpick and stand the frosted cake in the pie plate. Repeat with all 8 petits fours. Garnish with chopped nuts and bits of cherry. Makes 8. Freeze, unwrapped, until the frosting is firm. Then wrap and freeze until needed. They will defrost in the time it takes to prepare and serve the tea.

Chapter Five

A LIGHT DIET TEMPORARILY

There are times when even a well person needs soft foods temporarily. Maybe you are having some dental work done which makes active chewing practically impossible. That is no reason for meals to be tasteless. There are times when your doctor may suggest a light diet for a few days for any number of reasons, and these light meals should, if anything, be more attractive and tasty than ever in order to spur a picky eater to clean his plate.

Many a homemaker faced with the preparation of a light diet for her husband or herself assumes that this means two menus to plan and double meal preparation. You will find this couldn't be farther from the truth. Glance over the menus which follow. Serve such festive dishes as Polenta with Creamed Tuna* and Quiche Lorraine Custard* on a light diet! Of course you can! Long after there is no actual need to continue serving them you will find yourself voting to repeat more than one of these tasty dishes.

A light diet is merely one featuring easily digested, nutritious, fairly low-residue foods. You need adequate protein, minerals, vitamins and energy foods the same as ever. If you are instructed to omit some pungent spices temporarily, there are plenty of innocent herbs and extracts to add flavor and aroma.

MENUS

I

BREAKFAST

Applesauce
Cinnamon Milk Toast*
Tea or Hot Chocolate

LUNCH

Small Glass of Pineapple Juice
Corn Pudding with Diced Ham*
Buttered Canned Tiny Peas
Floating Island*
Tea   Milk

DINNER

Creamy Chicken Hash*
Escalloped Potatoes for Two*
Canned Peaches with Cinnamon Sour Cream*
Tea   Milk

II

BREAKFAST

Stewed Mixed Dried Fruits
Quick-cooking Cereal
French Toast   Honey or Jelly
Milk   Coffee or Tea

LUNCH

Oyster Stew* with Crackers
Canned Peach and Banana Salad
with Honey-Cheese Dressing*
Sponge Cake or Pound Cake Slice with
Quick Custard Sauce*
Tea

DINNER

Cup of Hot Tomato Juice
Salmon Loaf Supreme*
Whipped Potatoes
Bread   Butter or Margarine
Vanilla Pudding with Crushed Pineapple
Milk   Tea

III

BREAKFAST

Orange Juice
Poached Egg on Creamy Toast
(Toast softened with hot cream)
Hot Chocolate

LUNCH

Cream of Pea Soup   Crackers
Cottage Cheese and Peach Aspic*
Ice Cream   Cupcake
Milk   Tea

DINNER

Escalloped Sweetbreads*
Mashed Sweet Potatoes
Roll   Butter or Margarine
Grape Gelatin Dessert
Sugar Cookie
Tea   Milk

IV

BREAKFAST

Kadota Figs with Cream
Oatmeal with Brown Sugar and Milk
Tea or Hot Chocolate

LUNCH

Chicken Noodle Soup   Crackers
Baked Eggs Florentine*
Corn Muffins   Butter or Margarine
Sherbet   Sponge Cake
Milk   Tea

DINNER

Tomato Juice
Tarragon Fillets of Sole*
Buttered Rice
Chopped Canned Wax Beans in Cream
Bread   Butter or Margarine
Caramel Tapioca Pudding*
Tea   Milk

V

BREAKFAST

Apricot and Pineapple Juice
Scrambled Eggs
Blueberry Muffins Butter or Margarine
Milk Coffee or Tea

LUNCH

Consommé Crackers
Quiche Lorraine Custard*
Creamed Grated Carrots*
Individual Mocha Icebox Cakes*
Milk Tea

DINNER

Baked Chicken Livers with Chives*
Baked Potato
Buttered Summer Squash in Tomato Juice*
Banana Cream Pudding
(from a package mix)
Tea Milk

VI

BREAKFAST

Applesauce
Cream of Wheat
Puffy Omelet for Two*
Buttered Toast   Jelly
Coffee or Tea   Milk

LUNCH

Chicken Broth   Crackers
Escalloped Noodles with Mushroom
Creamed Peas*
Prune Whip for Two*
Milk   Tea

DINNER

Vegetable Juice Cocktail
Broiled Halibut with Dill Sauce*
Riced Potatoes
Buttered Canned Asparagus Spears
Roll   Butter or Margarine
Peach Bavarian*
Tea   Milk

VII

BREAKFAST

Sliced Bananas with Cream
Shirred Eggs with Minced Ham on Toast*
Tea or Coffee   Milk

LUNCH

Cream of Tomato Soup   Crackers
Cottage Cheese and Pear Salad
Buttered Toast
Baked Rice Cup Custard*
Hot Chocolate or Milk
Tea

DINNER

Jellied Consommé   Crackers
Polenta with Creamed Tuna*
Buttered Chopped Spinach
Chocolate Pudding
Tea   Milk

RECIPES

CINNAMON MILK TOAST

1½ cups milk	*2 to 3 slices buttered toast*
1 teaspoon butter or	*2 teaspoons sugar*
margarine	*Dash cinnamon*

In a small saucepan heat the milk and butter until tiny bubbles begin to form around the edge of the pan. Meanwhile, make toast, butter it and sprinkle with the sugar and cinnamon. Cut slices of toast in half and place half of it in each of two cereal bowls. Pour the hot milk over the toast and let it "steep" a minute until softened. Makes 2 servings.

CORN PUDDING WITH DICED HAM

2 eggs	*¼ teaspoon salt*
1¼ cups milk	*2 slices packaged boiled*
1 4½-ounce jar strained	*ham, diced, or ¼ cup*
creamed corn	*finely diced baked ham*

Heat oven to 325° F. Beat eggs. Add the remaining ingredients. Blend well. Grease a 3- or 4-cup baking dish. Pour the corn mixture into the baking dish and set it in a larger pan filled with 1 inch of hot water. Bake, uncovered, in preheated oven for 45 to 50 minutes or until a knife, inserted in the center, comes out clean. Serve hot. Makes 2 servings.

FLOATING ISLAND

½ package vanilla pudding
  mix (*not the instant*)
1¼ cups milk, or ¾ cup
  evaporated milk and ½
  cup water

1 egg
2 tablespoons sugar
Raspberry or currant jelly

Combine the pudding mix and milk in a small saucepan. Cook over low heat, stirring constantly, until just bubbling. Remove from heat. Break egg white into a small bowl. Set aside. Beat the yolk into the hot pudding, blending well. Pour it into 2 to 3 custard cups. Heat the oven to 450° F. Beat the egg white until stiff but not dry. Add the sugar, 1 tablespoon at a time, continuing to beat until the meringue is very stiff. Spoon a mound of it on top of each pudding; place custard cups on a cookie sheet and brown the meringue in preheated oven for 2 minutes. Serve warm, topped with a blob of jelly. Makes 2 to 3 servings.

CREAMY CHICKEN HASH

½ cup milk
2 tablespoons nonfat dry
  milk (*optional*)
1 teaspoon flour
½ teaspoon grated lemon
  rind
Dash salt
Dash pepper

1 teaspoon grated onion
1 cup finely diced cooked
  chicken, or 1 6-ounce
  can boneless chicken,
  minced
1 tablespoon grated
  Parmesan cheese

In a saucepan blend together milk, dry milk powder, flour, lemon rind, salt, pepper and onion. Add chicken and cook, stirring, over low heat until the sauce bubbles and is slightly thickened. Serve sprinkled with the grated cheese. Makes 2 servings.

ESCALLOPED POTATOES FOR TWO

¾ cup milk
2 cups pared, thinly sliced
  raw potatoes
1 tablespoon grated onion
1 tablespoon flour

¼ teaspoon salt
Dash pepper
1 tablespoon butter or
  margarine
Paprika

Heat oven to 375° F. In a small saucepan heat the milk until small bubbles form around the edge of the pan. Arrange half of the potatoes over the bottom of a well-greased 3- to 4-cup casserole. Sprinkle with half of the onion. Combine the flour, salt and pepper. Sprinkle half of the mixture over the potatoes in the pan. Dot with half of the butter. Repeat layers. Pour milk over all and sprinkle with paprika. Cover. Bake in preheated oven for 45 minutes. Remove cover; bake for another 10 minutes or until potatoes are very tender and lightly browned. Makes 2 servings.

CINNAMON SOUR CREAM

2 teaspoons sugar
⅛ teaspoon ground cinnamon
¼ cup commercial sour cream

Blend together sugar and cinnamon. Stir it into the sour cream, blending well. Serve seasoned sour cream over canned peach halves or other fruit. Makes 2 servings.

OYSTER STEW

1¼ cups half milk half
cream,[1] or ¾ cup
evaporated milk plus ½
cup water
1 7-ounce can oysters,
undrained

Salt and pepper to taste
Paprika
Oyster crackers

Heat the milk and cream in a saucepan until small bubbles begin to form around the edge of the pan. Add the oysters, juice and all. Heat slowly until steaming hot. Do not boil. Season to taste with salt and pepper. Sprinkle with paprika. Serve with oyster crackers. Makes 2 servings.

[1] For oyster stew low in fat and high in protein substitute 1¼ cups milk and ¼ cup nonfat dry milk for the half milk half cream.

HONEY-CHEESE DRESSING

¼ cup cottage cheese
1 tablespoon honey
¼ teaspoon grated lemon
rind

Dash powdered ginger
½ teaspoon dried parsley
flakes
Milk

In a small bowl mash the cottage cheese well. Add honey, lemon rind, ginger and parsley. Blend in enough milk (about 1 tablespoon) to make a creamy dressing. Makes about ¼ cup or enough dressing for 2 salads.

QUICK CUSTARD SAUCE

Prepare 1 package of vanilla pudding mix (not instant) as package directs. Chill. For custard sauce for two, thin half of the pudding with ½ cup light cream or milk. Beat it smooth. Pour the unthinned half of the pudding into a bowl and chill to use topped with fruits or chocolate sauce another day. Keep any unused sauce in a small jar in the refrigerator and use within a few days.

SALMON LOAF SUPREME

1 6¾-ounce can salmon,
  undrained
1 cup soft bread crumbs
1 egg
¼ cup milk
1 teaspoon parsley flakes

½ teaspoon instant minced
  onion
½ teaspoon salt
Dash pepper
Lemon wedges

Heat the oven to 375° F. Empty salmon, juice and all, into a bowl. Break it up with a fork. Add crumbs. With a fork beat the egg, milk, parsley flakes, onion, salt and pepper. Stir into the salmon in the bowl. Grease a 7½×3½×2½-inch loaf pan or a small baking dish (about 1 pint capacity). Spoon the salmon mixture into the pan. Bake in preheated oven for 30 minutes or until firm to the touch. Serve with lemon wedges. Makes 2 to 3 servings.

COTTAGE CHEESE AND PEACH ASPIC

One package of orange-flavored gelatin makes 2 servings of this aspic plus enough gelatin mixture for Peach Bavarian* to serve at another meal. See Dinner Menu VI.

1¾ cups cold water
3 whole cloves
1 envelope orange-flavored
  gelatin

¼ cup cottage cheese
2 well-drained canned peach
  halves
Lettuce leaves (optional)

In a small saucepan combine 1 cup of the water and the cloves. Bring to a boil. Pour over gelatin in a bowl and stir until it is dissolved. Stir in the remaining cold water. Spoon 2 tablespoons of the liquid into each of 2 6-ounce custard cups. Set the custard cups and the rest of the gelatin in the refrigerator until slightly thickened. Remove the cloves. Spoon half of the cottage cheese into the hollow center of each peach half. Arrange them over the gelatin layer in the custard cups. Fill cups with gelatin mixture. Chill until firm. Unmold and serve, if desired, on lettuce leaves. Makes 2 servings.

Meanwhile, while remaining gelatin is still only slightly thickened, prepare Peach Bavarian* for another meal.

ESCALLOPED SWEETBREADS

½ *pound sweetbreads*[2]
½ *teaspoon salt*
1 *tablespoon lemon juice*
6 *canned asparagus spears,*
  drained
1 *tablespoon pimiento strips*
⅔ *cup canned condensed*
  cream of mushroom soup,
  undiluted

2 *tablespoons sherry*
  (optional)
2 *to 4 tablespoons milk*
¼ *cup cracker crumbs*
2 *teaspoons melted butter*
  or margarine

In a large saucepan bring 1 quart of water to a boil. Add sweetbreads, salt and lemon juice. Bring to a boil; turn heat low; simmer, covered, for 20 minutes. Drain. Plunge sweetbreads into cold water. Remove the membrane and cut them into uniform pieces.

Heat oven to 375° F. Layer sweetbreads, asparagus and pimiento into 2 individual ramekins or a 3-cup casserole. In a small saucepan bring to a boil the soup, sherry and milk.

(If omitting sherry use 4 tablespoons of milk. If using it, use 2 tablespoons of milk.) Pour the sauce over the mixture in the ramekins. Sprinkle with cracker crumbs and drizzle with melted butter. Bake in preheated oven for 15 to 20 minutes or until sauce is bubbling hot. Makes 2 servings.

2 Sweetbreads are most frequently purchased in packages of about 1 pound each. Cook the whole pound. Divide it in half. Cool one half thoroughly; wrap for freezing and freeze for use another day.

BAKED EGGS FLORENTINE

¼ of a 10-ounce package frozen chopped spinach	2 teaspoons flour
	Dash salt
2 teaspoons light cream	Dash pepper
1 tablespoon melted butter	⅓ cup milk
3 tablespoons finely chopped Swiss cheese	2 eggs
	Paprika

Heat oven to 350° F. Lightly grease 2 6-ounce custard cups. Cook spinach as package label directs. Drain *well* in a coarse sieve, pressing out any excess liquid with the back of a spoon. Stir the cream and half of the butter into the spinach. Divide it evenly between the 2 custard cups. Sprinkle with half of the cheese. Blend the remaining melted butter, flour, salt and pepper in a small saucepan. Gradually stir in milk. Cook, stirring, until the sauce is smooth and thickened.

Carefully break the eggs over the spinach layers; cover them with sauce. Sprinkle with remaining cheese. Bake in preheated oven for 15 minutes. Sprinkle with paprika. Makes 2 servings.

TARRAGON FILLETS OF SOLE

2 small fillets of sole or 1
large fillet cut in half
(about ¾ pound)
1 tablespoon melted butter
or margarine

1 teaspoon lemon juice
Salt
¼ teaspoon dried tarragon
leaves
½ teaspoon chopped chives

Heat oven to 350° F. Wipe fillets with a damp paper towel. Arrange them in a shallow baking pan. Brush with melted butter. Drizzle with lemon juice and sprinkle lightly with salt. Bake in preheated oven for 20 minutes or until fish is just beginning to flake easily when tested with a fork. Sprinkle with tarragon and chives. Bake another 5 minutes. Makes 2 servings.

CARAMEL TAPIOCA PUDDING

1 egg
3 tablespoons minute
tapioca
¼ cup brown sugar, packed
1 teaspoon butter or
margarine

⅛ teaspoon salt
¾ cup evaporated milk
¾ cup water (or use 1½
cups milk instead of half
evaporated milk and half
water)

Beat egg. In a saucepan combine egg and remaining ingredients. Cook over low heat, stirring constantly, until mixture comes to a full boil. Pour into dessert dishes. Serve warm or chilled. Makes 2 to 3 servings.

QUICHE LORRAINE CUSTARD

Traditionally, a Quiche Lorraine is an elegant, one-crust pie. Swiss cheese is always an ingredient. Usually, too, you will find bacon bits and onion rings. Served either as an appetizer or as a luncheon main course, it is reserved for very special occasions. Without its rich pastry crust, Quiche Lorraine Custard is as tempting a light main dish as you could possibly concoct.

1 strip bacon
2 egg yolks
1 egg white
½ teaspoon instant minced
  onion
Dash salt

Dash nutmeg
½ cup shredded Swiss
  cheese
¾ cup milk
2 tablespoons nonfat dry
  milk (optional)

Heat oven to 350° F. Fry bacon crisp. Drain it on a paper towel and crumble it into small bits. Beat together the egg yolks and egg white; add bacon bits and remaining ingredients. Divide the mixture evenly between 2 6-ounce custard cups. Set them in a 9-inch pie plate. Pour 1 inch of hot water around them. Bake in preheated oven for 30 to 35 minutes or until puffed and lightly browned on top. Serve warm. Makes 2 servings.

CREAMED GRATED CARROTS

1½ cups shredded raw
  carrots
1 teaspoon butter or
  margarine

½ teaspoon flour
3 tablespoons milk
Salt

In a small saucepan cook carrots in boiling salted water to cover for 5 minutes or until just tender. Drain. Return to the saucepan. Stir in butter, flour and milk. Cook, stirring gently, until thickened and bubbling hot. Season to taste with salt. Makes 2 servings.

BAKED CHICKEN LIVERS WITH CHIVES

½ pound chicken livers   *2 tablespoons melted butter*
1 tablespoon flour   *1 teaspoon chopped chives*
⅛ teaspoon salt

Heat oven to 375° F. Drain chicken livers on paper towels. Combine flour and salt in a pie plate. Roll livers in flour mixture, coating them well. Arrange them in a well-greased shallow baking pan. Drizzle with melted butter. Bake in preheated oven 10 to 12 minutes or to the desired doneness. Serve sprinkled with chives. Makes 2 generous servings.

BUTTERED SUMMER SQUASH IN TOMATO JUICE

1 small yellow-neck squash   *⅓ cup tomato juice*
2 teaspoons butter or   *Salt*
* margarine*

Wash squash and slice it in ¼-inch slices. Cook it in boiling salted water to cover until tender but firm. Drain. In a saucepan combine squash, butter and tomato juice. Cook over medium heat until tomato juice is reduced to about 2 tablespoons. Season to taste with salt. Makes 2 servings.

PUFFY OMELET FOR TWO

3 eggs, separated
3 tablespoons water
¼ teaspoon salt

1 tablespoon shortening or
vegetable oil

Heat oven to 350° F. Put egg whites in one bowl and yolks in another. Add water to the egg whites and beat until stiff but not dry. Beat the yolks with salt until lemon-colored. Lightly fold the yolks into the egg whites, blending gently but well. Heat shortening in a 7- or 8-inch skillet. Tip the pan to make sure the bottom is well greased. Pour in the egg mixture. Cook over very low heat until well puffed and golden brown on the underside when gently lifted at the edge with a spatula. Then bake in preheated oven about 15 minutes or until the surface feels dry and the omelet springs back when gently pressed in the center.

Quickly run a spatula around the inside of the skillet to loosen the omelet. Cut down the center part way through. Fold one half over the other. Turn out onto a serving platter. Makes 2 servings.

ESCALLOPED NOODLES WITH MUSHROOM CREAMED PEAS

ESCALLOPED NOODLES

1½ cups packaged noodles
1 teaspoon melted butter
1 egg
¼ cup milk

Dash salt
1 teaspoon minced onion
1 teaspoon chopped parsley

Heat oven to 350° F. Thoroughly grease 2 6-ounce custard cups. Cook noodles in boiling salted water to cover until tender, about 6 minutes. Drain well. Pour melted butter over noodles and toss with a fork to coat them well. Beat egg with milk and salt. Stir in onion and parsley. Blend in noodles. Turn mixture into the 2 custard cups. Set cups in a pie plate; pour 1 inch of hot water into the pan around the custard cups. Bake for 30 minutes or until lightly browned. Unmold onto serving plates. Serve with Mushroom Creamed Peas. Makes 2 servings.

MUSHROOM CREAMED PEAS

2 tablespoons milk	Dash onion salt
½ cup canned condensed cream of mushroom soup, undiluted	½ cup canned tiny peas, drained

In a small saucepan blend together milk, soup and onion salt. Heat slowly, stirring constantly, until sauce is hot. Add peas. Heat. Makes 2 servings.

BROILED HALIBUT WITH DILL SAUCE

1 slice fresh or defrosted frozen halibut, about ¾ pound	3 tablespoons commercial sour cream
1 teaspoon lemon juice	¼ teaspoon grated lemon rind
1 teaspoon melted butter	½ teaspoon dried dill weed
Salt	

Heat oven to 375° F. Arrange fish in a shallow baking dish. Brush it with lemon juice and drizzle with melted butter. Sprinkle lightly with salt. Bake in preheated oven for 15 to 20 minutes or until fish flakes easily when tested with a fork. Combine sour cream, lemon rind and dill. Spread cream mixture over halibut. Broil 5 inches from source of heat for a minute or two or until sour cream begins to brown. Makes 2 servings.

PEACH BAVARIAN

*1 envelope whipped topping
mix*[3]

½ cup very cold milk

½ teaspoon vanilla extract

*½ of the slightly thickened
orange-flavored gelatin*[4]

2 ladyfingers

Prepare whipped topping mix as label directs, using the cold milk and vanilla extract. Pour thickened gelatin into a bowl. Blend in ½ cup of the whipped topping. Beat gently until mixture is thoroughly blended. Pour it into 2 6-ounce custard cups. Split ladyfingers apart and cut them in half crosswise. Arrange them around the edge of the Bavarian cream. Chill until ready to serve. Makes 2 servings. They will keep for several days in the refrigerator for another meal's dessert.

Drop the leftover whipped topping in serving-sized blobs over the bottom of a pie plate. Freeze, unwrapped, until firm. Then put them into a small plastic bag; seal; freeze for use later.

[3] Or, instead of prepared whipped topping mix, use ½ cup whipped cream.
[4] See Cottage Cheese and Peach Aspic.*

SHIRRED EGGS WITH MINCED HAM

*¼ cup milk or half milk
and half cream*

*¼ cup ground ham (ready-
to-eat or leftover baked),
or 2 slices boiled ham,
minced*

2 eggs

Dash salt

Paprika

Heat oven to 375° F. Grease 2 shirred-egg dishes or custard cups. Pour half of the milk into each. Sprinkle in the ham, dividing it equally between the two dishes. Break in the eggs. Sprinkle with salt and paprika. Bake in preheated oven for about 10 minutes, or until eggs are firm enough to suit your taste. Serve piping hot. Makes 2 servings.

BAKED RICE CUP CUSTARD

1 egg, slightly beaten
Dash salt
3 tablespoons sugar
1 cup milk

¾ teaspoon vanilla extract
3 tablespoons cooked rice
Dash nutmeg

Heat oven to 350° F. Beat egg with salt, sugar, milk and vanilla just until well blended. Stir in rice. Turn mixture into 2 6-ounce ungreased custard cups. Sprinkle with nutmeg. Set custard cups in a pan containing 1 inch of hot water; bake in preheated oven for 30 to 35 minutes or until a knife inserted in the center comes out clean. Cool, then chill. Makes 2 servings.

POLENTA WITH CREAMED TUNA

POLENTA

2½ cups water
½ teaspoon salt
¾ cup yellow corn meal
1 egg, beaten
½ cup grated Cheddar
  cheese

1 teaspoon melted butter or
  margarine
1 tablespoon grated
  Parmesan cheese

In a heavy saucepan bring the water and salt to boiling. Slowly add corn meal, stirring constantly. Reduce heat; cook very slowly, uncovered, stirring frequently until the mixture is very thick and leaves the sides of the pan. Blend in the egg and Cheddar cheese. Stir until cheese is melted. Pour into a well-greased 7½ ×3½ ×2½ -inch loaf pan. Chill until the corn meal is thick enough to slice, about 1 hour.

With a small spatula loosen the corn meal and turn it out of the pan onto a pie plate. Slice off 4 1-inch-thick slices. Return the rest of the mush to the loaf pan; cover and refrigerate for another meal. Arrange the slices on a piece of foil. Drizzle them with butter and sprinkle with the Parmesan cheese. Run them under the broiler until heated through and slightly brown on top. Serve with Creamed Tuna. Makes 2 servings for today and 2 for another meal.

CREAMED TUNA

2 teaspoons butter or margarine
1 tablespoon all-purpose flour
¾ cup milk

1 teaspoon capers, drained
1 3½-ounce-can tuna, flaked
Salt and pepper to taste
Paprika

Melt butter in a small saucepan. Stir in flour. Gradually blend in milk, stirring constantly over low heat until sauce is smooth and bubbling. Add capers and tuna. Season to taste with salt and pepper. Serve over Polenta. Sprinkle with paprika. Makes 2 servings.

SLEEP-TIGHT NIGHTCAPS

If your light-dieter has been a bedtime nibbler and could use a little nourishment between dinnertime and breakfast, lull him to sleep with one of these easily digested nightcaps.

PRUNE NOG

⅔ cup bottled prune juice
1 teaspoon sugar
⅓ cup milk and 1 tablespoon nonfat dry milk, or ⅓ cup half milk half cream
Ground cinnamon

Pour prune juice into a tall glass. Stir in sugar and milk. Blend in nonfat dry milk. Sprinkle with cinnamon. Makes 1 glass.

BANANA EGGNOG

1 small, ripe banana
2 teaspoons sugar
¼ teaspoon vanilla extract

1 cup milk
1 egg
Grated nutmeg

Peel and mash the banana. Add the sugar and vanilla, half of the milk and the egg. Beat with an egg beater until blended. Stir in the rest of the milk. Pour into 2 glasses. Sprinkle with nutmeg. Makes 2 servings.

HOT SPICED GRAPE JUICE

1 cup grape juice
¼ teaspoon grated lemon
  rind
3 whole cloves

Small stick cinnamon (about
  1 inch long)
1 teaspoon sugar

Blend all ingredients in a small saucepan. Bring to a boil and simmer for 1 minute. Cool enough to drink with enjoyment. Strain into a mug or cup. Makes 1 serving.

HOT TEA PUNCH

1 tea bag
1 cup boiling water
2 teaspoons sugar

Dash ground ginger
½ cup hot milk

Place tea bag in a pitcher and pour boiling water over it. Let steep for 3 minutes. Remove tea bag. Add remaining ingredients. Makes 2 servings.

Chapter Six

MEALS IN MINUTES
FROM YOUR PANTRY SHELF

Someday it is going to happen to you! It does to everyone! All of a sudden, in spite of your careful marketing, you don't have the makings of a good dinner on hand! On top of that it is raining cats and dogs, or the sun is so hot you would rather starve than dash off to the supermarket.

Well, don't starve or get overheated or dash anywhere. Just use your "emergency dinner insurance" bought in advance of all emergencies and kept on your pantry shelf in the form of ingredients needed to serve several of the following menus. They are quick-to-prepare complete meals—not just heated up cans of this and that. All ingredients will wait on the shelf till their turn comes to make dinner a tasty one.

Keep a little butter or margarine in the freezer, since some of the recipes call for several teaspoons. Remember the advice in Chapter Two about buying a pound at supermarket sales figures? With part of the pound always frozen, *it* won't be the item you lack. Stock up on the other ingredients for at least two of these tasty meals. None of them are perishables and you can keep them for months. Then, rain or shine or unexpected guests or what not, who cares? You'll serve dinner as usual and a mighty good one.

Menu I

Fruit Juice Cocktail
Chicken and Noodle Bake*
Sweet and Sour Beets*
Ry-Krisp
Mocha Whip*
Tea or Coffee

Pantry Shelf Foods for Menu I

1 package noodles
Parsley flakes
Instant minced onion
1 can condensed cream of chicken soup
1 5½-ounce can boned chicken
1 8¼-ounce can sliced beets
Ground cinnamon
Ground cloves
Vinegar
Vegetable oil
A little cornstarch (you will need only 1 teaspoon, and
   you can substitute 2 to 3 teaspoons flour if need be)
1 small can of your favorite fruit juice
1 package Ry-Krisp
1 small jar instant coffee powder
1 package chocolate-flavored whipped dessert mix
A jar of powdered cream substitute, if you like it for tea
   or coffee
Tea or coffee (or instant nonfat dry milk powder to recon-
   stitute and drink as the beverage)

Recipes for Menu I

CHICKEN AND NOODLE BAKE

1½ quarts water
1 teaspoon salt
3 cups packaged noodles
1 teaspoon dried parsley
flakes
1 teaspoon instant minced
onion

½ cup canned condensed
cream of chicken soup,
undiluted
¼ cup water
1 5½-ounce can boned
chicken
Salt and pepper to taste
2 teaspoons butter or
margarine

Heat oven to 375° F. In a medium-sized saucepan bring water and salt to a rapid boil. Sprinkle in noodles. Cook over medium heat, uncovered, for 8 minutes. Drain well. In a 1-quart casserole combine noodles, parsley flakes, onion, soup and water. Gently stir in chicken. Season to taste with salt and pepper. Dot with butter. Bake in preheated oven for 15 minutes or until mixture is hot and just beginning to brown on top. Makes 2 generous servings.

SWEET AND SOUR BEETS

1 8¼-ounce can sliced beets
1 tablespoon sugar
Dash ground cinnamon
Dash ground cloves
2 tablespoons vinegar

2 teaspoons vegetable oil
Dash salt
1 teaspoon cornstarch or
2½ teaspoons flour

Drain beets, reserving liquid. In a small saucepan combine sugar, cinnamon, cloves, vinegar, oil, salt and cornstarch. Gradually blend in liquid from beets. Bring mixture to a boil over low heat, stirring constantly. Add beets and heat 1 minute. Serve hot. Makes 2 servings.

MOCHA WHIP

1 3¾-ounce package chocolate-flavored whipped dessert mix
1 teaspoon instant coffee powder

½ cup very cold milk
½ cup cold water

Empty package of whipped dessert mix into a small, deep bowl. Stir in powdered coffee. Using cold milk and water, whip, following package directions. Chill. Makes 3 to 4 servings. Keep unused servings in the refrigerator for later use.

Menu II

Escalloped Crab*
Canned Stewed Tomatoes
Crackers or Melba Toast
Canned Apricot Halves
Packaged Cookies
Tea or Coffee or Hot Chocolate
(made with nonfat dry or evaporated milk)

Pantry Shelf Foods for Menu II

1 7½-ounce can crab meat
1 can condensed cream of celery soup
Dried parsley flakes
Instant minced onion
Crisp crackers
1 10-ounce can stewed tomatoes
Melba toast
1 8¾-ounce can apricot halves
A package of your favorite cookies
Nonfat dry milk
Powdered chocolate (optional)

Recipe for Menu II

ESCALLOPED CRAB

1 7½-ounce can crab meat
½ cup canned condensed cream of celery soup, undiluted
1 teaspoon dried parsley flakes
½ teaspoon instant minced onion

½ cup coarsely crushed crisp cracker crumbs
Salt and pepper to taste
1 teaspoon melted butter or margarine

Heat oven to 375° F. Remove any bony tissue from crab. In a bowl combine crab, celery soup, parsley flakes, onion and crumbs. Season to taste with salt and pepper. Turn mixture into 2 ramekins or a 2-cup baking dish. Drizzle with melted butter. Bake in preheated oven for 15 minutes or until hot and lightly browned on top. Makes 2 servings.

Menu III

Spaghetti with Red Clam Sauce*
Asparagus Vinaigrette*
Packaged Bread Sticks
Grape Gelatin Dessert
Tea or Coffee

Pantry Shelf Foods for Menu III

½ of an 8-ounce package spaghetti
1 7½-ounce can minced clams
Garlic salt
Dried parsley flakes
Orégano or basil
1 8-ounce can tomato sauce
1 jar grated Parmesan cheese
1 10½-ounce can asparagus tips
1 bottle capers
Bottled French dressing
1 small jar pimiento or pimiento-stuffed olives
Dried parsley flakes
Garlic salt (optional)
1 package bread sticks
1 package grape gelatin dessert

Recipes for Menu III

SPAGHETTI WITH RED CLAM SAUCE

½ 8-ounce package spaghetti
1 7½-ounce can minced
  clams
⅛ teaspoon garlic salt
1 teaspoon dried parsley
  flakes

½ teaspoon orégano or basil
1 8-ounce can tomato sauce
Salt and pepper to taste
2 tablespoons grated
  Parmesan cheese

Cook spaghetti as label on package directs. Drain. Meanwhile make clam sauce. Drain clams, reserving juice. In a saucepan combine clam juice, garlic salt, parsley flakes, orégano or basil and tomato sauce. Bring mixture to a boil; turn heat low and simmer uncovered for 15 minutes. Stir in reserved clams. Heat. Season to taste with salt and pepper. Serve over spaghetti. Top with Parmesan cheese. Makes 2 generous servings.

ASPARAGUS VINAIGRETTE

1 10½-ounce can
  asparagus tips, drained
1 teaspoon capers
1 tablespoon chopped
  pimiento or chopped
  pimiento-stuffed olives

3 tablespoons bottled
  French dressing[1]
½ teaspoon dried parsley
  flakes
Dash garlic salt (*optional*)

Empty asparagus into a shallow dish. Combine remaining ingredients and pour over asparagus. Chill. Makes 2 servings.

[1] Instead of bottled French dressing use, if you prefer, 1 tablespoon vinegar, two tablespoons olive or vegetable oil and salt to taste.

Menu IV

Vegetable Juice Cocktail
Escalloped Potatoes and Sausages*
Creamed Peas and Carrots*
Melba Toast
Fruit Tapioca (Fruit Soup)*
Tea   Milk (from nonfat dry milk powder)

Pantry Shelf Foods for Menu IV

At least ½ of a 5⅝-ounce package oven-ready scalloped potatoes
1 4-ounce can Vienna sausages
1 8¼-ounce can peas and carrots
Some nonfat dry milk powder
At least 1 tablespoon tapioca
Ground cinnamon
A few tablespoons brown sugar
1 8¼-ounce can fruits for salad
1 8-ounce can vegetable juice cocktail
Melba toast

Recipes for Menu IV

ESCALLOPED POTATOES AND SAUSAGES

½ of a 5⅝-ounce package oven-ready scalloped potatoes
1½ cups boiling water
2 teaspoons butter or margarine
1 4-ounce can Vienna sausages, drained

Heat oven to 400° F. Empty contents of package of scalloped potatoes into a bowl. Stir well to mix potato slices and dry ingredients in the package. Measure 1½ cups (about half) of the potatoes and dry ingredients back into the original package; seal and return it to the pantry shelf for another meal. Empty remaining potato slices and dry mixture into a 3- to 4-cup casserole. Add the boiling water and butter. Stir once. Bake, uncovered, in preheated oven for 30 minutes. Arrange sausages over the potatoes in the casserole and continue to bake, uncovered, for 15 minutes. Makes 2 servings.

CREAMED PEAS AND CARROTS

1 8¼-ounce can peas and carrots
2 teaspoons butter or margarine
3 tablespoons nonfat dry milk powder
1 tablespoon flour
Salt and pepper to taste

Drain peas and carrots well, reserving liquid. Add water to the liquid, if necessary, to measure ½ cup. In a saucepan over medium heat melt butter. Stir in nonfat dry milk powder and flour, blending well, add reserved liquid. Cook, stirring constantly, until sauce is smooth and thickened. Add peas and carrots. Heat. Season to taste with salt and pepper. Makes 2 servings.

FRUIT TAPIOCA (Fruit Soup)

This favorite from Sweden, known there as fruit soup, is a traditional holiday favorite.

1 8¼-ounce can fruits for salad
2 tablespoons brown sugar
Dash salt
1 tablespoon tapioca
⅛ teaspoon ground cinnamon

Drain fruits, reserving juice. Add water to juice to make ¾ cup liquid. In a small saucepan combine brown sugar, salt, tapioca and cinnamon. Stir in juice. Cook over medium heat, stirring frequently, until the mixture comes to a full rolling boil. Remove from heat. Stir in drained fruits. Let stand 15 minutes. Stir well. Serve warm or chilled. Makes 2 servings.

Menu V

Shrimp and Rice Curry in a Hurry*
Chutney
Ripe Olives   Pickled Onions
Stewed Tomatoes or Canned Green Beans
Melba Rounds
Applesauce   Gingerbread
Tea or Coffee

Pantry Shelf Foods for Menu V

Curry powder
Dried parsley flakes
Instant minced onion
Long grain white rice (at least ½ cup)
1 5-ounce can shrimp
1 bottle chutney
1 small jar pickled onions
1 10-ounce can stewed tomatoes or canned green beans
Melba toast rounds
1 8-ounce jar applesauce
1 package gingerbread mix
Tea or coffee, and powdered cream substitute if needed

Recipe for Menu V

SHRIMP AND RICE CURRY IN A HURRY

*1½ teaspoons curry
powder*
1 cup water
*1 teaspoon dried parsley
flakes*
*1 teaspoon instant minced
onion*

¼ teaspoon salt
½ cup long grain white rice
*1 5-ounce can shrimp,
drained*

Measure the curry powder into a custard cup. Stir a little of the water into it, blending well. Combine curry, remaining water, parsley flakes, onion and salt in a saucepan with cover. Bring to a boil. Stir in rice. Bring to a boil again; cover; turn heat low and simmer about 20 minutes or until the moisture is absorbed and the rice tender and fluffy. Add shrimp. Mix lightly with a fork. Remove from heat. Cover and let stand 3 to 4 minutes or until shrimp are heated through. Add salt to taste, if necessary. Makes 2 generous servings.

Menu VI

Salmon and Vegetable Casserole*
Fluffy Rice
Marinated Artichoke Hearts
Biscuits from a Mix
Butter or Margarine
Sliced Peaches or Royal Ann Cherries
Date Bars
Tea or Coffee

Pantry Shelf Foods for Menu VI

1 7¾-ounce can salmon
1 8¼-ounce can mixed vegetables
1 6-ounce jar marinated artichoke hearts
1 can condensed tomato soup
Bottled lemon juice
Dried parsley flakes
Dried dill weed
A few saltine-type crackers
Biscuit mix
Nonfat dry milk for biscuits
1 8¾-ounce can sliced peaches or Royal Ann cherries
1 14-ounce package date bar mix
Tea or coffee and the powdered cream substitute if needed

Recipe for Menu VI

SALMON AND VEGETABLE CASSEROLE

1 7¾-ounce can salmon
1 8¼-ounce can mixed vegetables, drained
½ cup canned condensed tomato soup
1 teaspoon bottled lemon juice (or use fresh)
1 teaspoon dried parsley flakes

¼ teaspoon dried dill weed
⅛ teaspoon salt
Dash pepper
¼ cup crumbled saltine-type crackers
1 teaspoon butter or margarine

Heat oven to 375° F. Flake salmon and empty it into a 3-cup baking dish. Add vegetables, soup, lemon juice, parsley flakes, dill weed, salt and pepper. Blend lightly. Sprinkle with cracker crumbs and dot with butter. Bake in preheated oven for 15 minutes or until hot. Makes 2 servings.

Chapter Seven

MEALS FROM A
TABLE-TOP KITCHEN

If you decide to sell the big old house you have lived in for years and move into an easy-to-clean, efficiency-type studio room, you'll find you can turn out wonderful meals with almost no kitchen at all. You will need a refrigerator, and if one is not part of your new built-in equipment, you can install a tiny plug-in refrigerator finished in mahogany, walnut, etc., to fit in with your particular décor. These are no more conspicuous than a TV cabinet. Then, with a few electrical appliances set up on a 3-by-3 counter or even a teacart, you'll be in business to serve dinner as usual. You'll have no big kitchen floor to mop, almost no housework to tie you down!

To equip your capsule kitchen there are dozens of shining appliances—table-top broilers, some that do more than just broil, various sizes of table-top ovens, toasters, coffee makers, portable ranges (the modern term for what most of us have always called one- or two-burner hot plates), automatic frypans, mixers, blenders and can openers, to name a few. The important thing to remember is not to buy too many in a spurt of enthusiasm. Just a few will do. In fact a few at a time *have* to do if your electrical wiring is average. Better check with your superintendent to be sure just how many you may use at one time without blowing a fuse. The meals which follow use only one at a time, though several are used to complete the meals. With motor-driven appliances such as mixers, can openers and blenders it's different. These don't put as much of a load on your electrical current as do the cooking appliances, so several may be used simultaneously or in conjunction with a table oven, broiler or fry-pan.

Enjoy a bit of leisurely browsing before you settle on your counter equipment and select a minimum. You can always add more if you find you lack one you really would use often. You'll find appliances which you probably never dreamed existed. For instance, there is an instant coffee/tea brewer with which you can make either tea or coffee, and as little as 2 cups at a time. If you are a frozen-dinner-heater rather than an enthusiastic cook, there is a compartment food cooker which heats food and shuts off automatically when it is hot. It does not brown foods like an oven, but cooks frozen or fresh vegetables, heats frozen complete meals, and heats rolls and leftovers without a chance of burning them. Instructions which accompany your purchases are easy to follow and you'll want to keep them handy for daily reference.

For efficient, energy-saving devices treat yourself to a mixer (a portable one will do very well) and an electric can opener. What a great little labor-saving device that can opener is. Perhaps you won't need to buy all of this kitchen equipment. Drop a hint when Christmas or birthdays roll around. Aren't children and friends always trying to find out what they can give you that you really want?

Menu I

A tiny table oven (Redi-Baker) and a coffee maker prepare this pot roast dinner, and there will be roast left for sandwiches for another meal. Prepare the pot roast first. The Honey Graham Baked Bananas bake while you eat your main course. Then disconnect your oven and plug in your coffee maker. Coffee will be ready to serve in a few minutes—almost by the time you have served up the bananas. You can, if you prefer, make the coffee before baking the pot roast. When it cuts off to "hold" it uses much less electrical current.

Table Oven Pot Roast with Vegetables*
Packaged Rolls   Butter or Margarine
Lettuce and Tomato Salad   Thousand Island Dressing
Honey Graham Baked Bananas*
Glass of Milk
Coffee

TABLE OVEN POT ROAST WITH VEGETABLES

*1 pound round steak (a
piece about 3 inches by
5 inches and 1¼ inches
thick)*

*2 medium-sized potatoes
2 medium-sized carrots
½ package dry onion soup
mix*

Plug in your table oven. Turn the dial to 425° F. Place the round steak in the center of a piece of heavy-duty aluminum foil about 12 inches square. (Or use two thicknesses of regular aluminum foil.) Peel the potatoes and scrape the carrots. Slice potatoes in ½-inch slices and the carrots even thinner. Arrange vegetables around the meat on the foil and pour the dry soup over. Wrap meat and vegetables in foil, folding the edges to seal in the juices. Place the foil packet in the oven tray. Close oven and bake for 1¼ hours or until vegetables are done. Seasoned to perfection with the soup, the meat has plenty of onion-flavored natural gravy. Makes 2 servings, plus meat for another meal.

HONEY GRAHAM BAKED BANANAS

*2 small, firm bananas
2 tablespoons honey
1 tablespoon packaged
graham cracker crumbs[1]*

*1 teaspoon butter or
margarine
Ground cinnamon*

Heat the table oven to 425° F. Peel bananas and place them on a square of aluminum foil. Crimp the edges of the foil up around the sides of the bananas to hold in the juices. Drizzle bananas with honey. Sprinkle with crumbs and dot with butter. Place foil "baking dish" with bananas in the oven. Close the oven and bake for 8 to 10 minutes. Serve warm, sprinkled with cinnamon. Makes 2 servings.

1 Or crumble about ½ of a graham cracker.

Menu II

A table broiler goes to work to prepare stuffed hamburgers, potato patties and tomato halves for this dinner. Make the dessert ahead of time—at least 2 hours before dinner. If using an automatic coffee maker, perk the coffee while you eat the main course. If you prefer tea and have no portable range (hot plate) on which to boil the water, you may want to invest in the 2- to 5-cup instant coffee/tea brewer.

Broiled Stuffed Burgers*
Broil-Browned Frozen Potato Patties*
Grilled Tomato Halves*
Rolls or Bread
Butter or Margarine
Orange and Grapefruit Salad
French Dressing
Freezer Tray Ice Cream Pudding*
Glass of Milk
Tea or Coffee

BROILED STUFFED BURGERS

½ *pound lean ground beef*
1 *teaspoon instant minced*
 onion

1 *slice packaged American*
 cheese
Salt and pepper

Plug in table broiler. Slide rack in position about 5 inches from heat. Combine beef and onion. Divide the mixture into 4 equal portions. Form each into a thin, round patty. Cut the slice of cheese in half and fold each piece in two to form a small square of cheese. Place cheese squares in the center of two of the beef patties. Top with the two remaining patties and mold the edges together, sealing in the cheese. Sprinkle with salt and pepper. Arrange patties on a piece of foil or in a shallow foil pan. Place them on the rack in the heated broiler. Broil for about 7 minutes on each side, or to desired doneness. Makes 2 servings.

BROIL-BROWNED FROZEN POTATO PATTIES

2 *frozen packaged potato patties*
Salt and pepper
Paprika or dried parsley flakes

Arrange frozen patties in a shallow, disposable aluminum pan or on a sheet of foil. Sprinkle them with salt and pepper. Place on the broiler rack about 5 inches from heat, and heat for 8 to 10 minutes or until sizzling hot, turning occasionally to brown both sides. Serve sprinkled with paprika or parsley flakes. Drizzle with juices from Broiled Stuffed Burgers.* Makes 2 servings.

GRILLED TOMATO HALVES

1 large, ripe tomato
Salt and pepper
Sprinkling of dry mustard

1 teaspoon butter or
margarine

Cut tomato in half crosswise. Sprinkle cut surfaces lightly with salt, pepper and mustard. Dot with butter; arrange on a sheet of foil and broil 5 inches from heat for about 8 minutes or until hot and fork-tender. Makes 2 servings.

FREEZER TRAY ICE CREAM PUDDING

½ pint vanilla ice cream
4 packaged fig bars, crumbled
½ teaspoon grated orange rind[2]

Soften ice cream slightly. Pack half of it into an empty ice cube tray. Sprinkle it with the crumbled fig bars and the orange rind. Pack the rest of the ice cream over the crumb layer. Place in the freezing compartment of the refrigerator for at least 1 hour before serving. Makes 2 generous servings.

[2] If you aren't already familiar with the packaged-in-jars grated orange rind, you'll find it a fine, energy-saving, no-waste pantry shelf item to keep on hand.

Menu III

An automatic fry-pan, coffee maker and blender make this dinner preparation easy. Actually, you don't have to have a blender to prepare it. If you don't have one, substitute packaged strawberry ice cream for the Blender Strawberry Ice Cream.*

Asparagus Soup Shake*
Meatballs with Spanish Rice*
Peach and Cottage Cheese Salad
Packaged Corn Muffins   Butter or Margarine
Blender Strawberry Ice Cream*
Coffee

ASPARAGUS SOUP SHAKE[3]

*1 10½-ounce can cream of
    asparagus soup
1 soup can of cold milk*

*½ teaspoon minced chives
2 lemon wedges*

Combine soup and milk in your electric blender. Cover and turn to low speed. Blend for 15 seconds. (Or shake in a pitcher or shaker with tight-fitting cover.) Pour it into 2 tall tumblers. Sprinkle with chives and serve with a wedge of lemon.

[3] This tasty drink can double as a first course and a milk beverage.

MEATBALLS WITH SPANISH RICE

*¼ pound ground lean beef
½ teaspoon salt
Dash pepper
1 slice bread
1 egg, beaten
1 tablespoon catsup
2 tablespoons vegetable oil
    or shortening*

*¼ cup frozen minced
    green pepper or ½
    small green pepper,
    seeded and diced
1 small onion, thinly sliced
½ cup raw regular white
    rice
1 cup tomato juice
1 cup water
¼ teaspoon salt
1 teaspoon chili powder*

Combine beef, the ½ teaspoon salt and pepper in a bowl. Tear bread into crumbs. Add crumbs, egg and catsup to meat. Blend well and form into 6 small balls. Heat fry-pan to 350° F. Heat oil in pan and brown meatballs, turning to brown all sides well. Add green pepper and onion. Turn heat to 250° F. and cook vegetables for 2 minutes. Then add rice, tomato juice, water, remaining salt and chili powder. Stir and cover the pan. Cook 20 to 25 minutes or until rice is tender and fluffy. (Check moisture from time to time and add a little more water if rice begins to stick to the pan before it is tender). Makes 2 generous servings.

BLENDER STRAWBERRY ICE CREAM

1 10-ounce package frozen strawberries, defrosted

1 14-ounce can sweetened condensed milk

2 tablespoons lime or lemon juice

1 teaspoon grated lemon rind

1 cup heavy cream, whipped

Set control of refrigerator at coldest setting. Pour defrosted berries into blender. Cover and blend at high speed for 20 seconds, or until smooth. Turn speed to low; remove cover; pour condensed milk in a steady stream into berries. Stir in juice and rind. Fold mixture into whipped cream. Pour it into a 1-quart mold or plastic container. Cover. Freeze at least 3 hours or until firm. Makes 1 quart.

Menu IV

A toaster and portable range (hot plate) prepare this dinner in a jiffy. Prepare the Tuna and Vegetable Rabbit first.

Heat water for tea. Disconnect the portable range and plug in the toaster. Toast will be golden brown by the time the tea has steeped.

Small Glass of Grape Juice
Tuna and Vegetable Rabbit on Toast*
Carrot and Raisin Slaw*
Bread or Rolls
Butter or Margarine
Frozen Ice Cream Cake Roll (from your supermarket)
Glass of Milk   Tea

TUNA AND VEGETABLE RABBIT ON TOAST

*1 tablespoon butter or
  margarine*
1 tablespoon flour
*1 cup milk or ½ cup
  each evaporated milk
  and water*
*½ cup grated Cheddar
  cheese*

¼ teaspoon salt
*¼ teaspoon powdered
  mustard*
1 3½-ounce can tuna
*½ cup canned peas or
  cooked mixed vegetables,
  drained*
2 to 3 slices buttered toast

Melt butter in a saucepan. Add flour and blend. Stir in milk and cook over low heat, stirring constantly until thick. Add cheese and seasonings. Stir until cheese is melted, about 1 minute. Stir in tuna and peas or vegetables. Serve hot over buttered toast. Makes 2 generous servings.

CARROT AND RAISIN SLAW

½ cup shredded cabbage
½ cup grated raw carrot
   (*1 small*)
2 tablespoons seedless
   raisins

Dash salt
1 tablespoon lemon juice
1½ teaspoons sugar
2 tablespoons mayonnaise

Lightly toss cabbage, carrot, raisins, salt, lemon juice and sugar until well combined. Chill until ready to serve. Just before serving toss with mayonnaise. Makes 2 servings.

Menu V

Serve this complete meal if your total kitchen consists of no more equipment than an electric hot plate (a portable range). Even one with a single burner will do.

Beef Stew with Noodles*
Tossed Green Salad   Russian Dressing
Bread   Butter or Margarine
Lemon Chiffon Pie for Two*
Tea   Glass of Milk

BEEF STEW WITH NOODLES

¾ pound beef chuck, cut
   in 1-inch pieces
1 tablespoon shortening
2½ cups water
½ teaspoon Worcestershire
   sauce
1 small clove garlic, peeled

1 small onion, sliced
1 bay leaf
½ teaspoon salt
¼ teaspoon pepper
1½ cups packaged noodles
½ teaspoon caraway seeds
   (*optional*)

In a heavy skillet or saucepan with tight-fitting cover, brown meat well on all sides in shortening. Add water, Worcestershire sauce, garlic, onion, bay leaf, salt and pepper. Cover pan and simmer for 1½ hours or until meat is very tender. Add a little more water from time to time, if necessary, to keep plenty of liquid boiling around the beef. Pour in the noodles and caraway seeds. Continue to cook for 10 minutes. Makes 2 generous servings.

LEMON CHIFFON PIE FOR TWO

1 tablespoon cold water	3 tablespoons lemon juice
1 teaspoon unflavored	Dash salt
gelatine	½ teaspoon grated lemon
1 egg	rind
4 tablespoons sugar	12 packaged vanilla wafers

Measure the cold water into a custard cup and sprinkle the gelatine over it. Let stand. Separate egg. Combine the yolk, 2 tablespoons of the sugar, the lemon juice, salt and lemon rind in the top of a double boiler. Beat with a spoon to blend. Set the top of the double boiler over boiling water and cook the mixture, stirring constantly, until smooth and slightly thickened, about 5 minutes. Stir in the softened gelatine. Remove from heat. Beat egg white until stiff but not dry. Gradually beat in the remaining sugar, beating until the meringue is stiff and glossy. Fold it into the hot lemon mixture. Line the bottom and sides of 2 8-ounce glass baking dishes with wafers. Pour the lemon chiffon into the cookie crusts and chill. If made the same day, chill at least 1½ hours. Makes 2 generous servings.

Menu VI

An automatic fry-pan is the appliance featured here. Or you may just as well use a skillet with a tight-fitting cover on top of a one-burner portable range.

Cranberry Juice Cocktail
Skillet Chicken and Rice Pilaf*
Two-Meal Vegetable Aspic*
Mayonnaise
Rolls or Bread   Butter or Margarine
Lime Sherbet   Packaged Cookies
Milk   Tea

SKILLET CHICKEN AND RICE PILAF

3 tablespoons butter, margarine or vegetable oil
2 medium-sized chicken legs (drumsticks and thighs)
Salt and pepper
½ cup water
½ cup raw regular white rice

2 tablespoons instant minced onion
½ teaspoon orégano
¼ teaspoon salt
1 13¾-ounce can chicken broth (about 1¾ cups)
2 tablespoons toasted slivered almonds (optional)

Heat automatic fry-pan to 350° F. Melt butter. Add chicken; sprinkle it with salt and pepper. Brown chicken lightly on both sides. Turn heat to simmer. Cover pan and cook for 10 minutes. Add the water. Cover the pan again and continue to cook until chicken is almost tender, about

15 minutes longer. Add rice. Pour enough water into broth to make 2 cups liquid. Add broth and remaining ingredients to chicken and rice in pan. Cover and simmer for 20 to 25 minutes or until moisture is absorbed and rice is fluffy. Stir in almonds, if desired. Makes 2 generous servings.

TWO-MEAL VEGETABLE ASPIC

1 3-ounce package salad gelatin mix (Italian flavor)
1 cup very hot water
2 teaspoons vinegar
⅔ cup cold water
1 large carrot, scraped and shredded (about 1 cup)

2 tablespoons finely chopped onion
1 tablespoon dried parsley flakes
1 5½-ounce can boned chicken, diced
Lettuce leaves
Mayonnaise

Empty gelatin mix into a medium-sized bowl. Add the hot water and stir until the gelatin is dissolved. Add vinegar and cold water. Chill until it is the consistency of unbeaten egg whites. Stir in carrot, onion and parsley. Fill 2 individual molds with the gelatin mixture or fill 2 6-ounce custard cups two-thirds full. Chill. Stir chicken into the rest of the gelatin mixture. Pour it into a 2- to 3-cup mold. Chill. Unmold the individual salads on lettuce leaves and serve with mayonnaise for dinner with Skillet Chicken and Rice Pilaf.* Keep the larger mold of chicken and vegetables refrigerated for a luncheon main-dish salad another day. Makes 2 servings for 2 different meals. Keeps refrigerated for 3 to 4 days.

Chapter Eight

FOR CALORIE WATCHERS

For the full enjoyment of these retirement years, you know you are going to be watching your weight. Everyone does if he is smart—fat, medium or slim. Once those murderous pounds disappear, you'll feel and look years younger. Only dinner menus appear here because while you are losing weight, breakfast with citrus fruit, a lightly buttered piece of toast and an egg can be pretty standard and adequate. A cup of soup with a few crackers, a salad with a low-calorie dressing and a glass of milk (preferably fat free milk—skim milk, buttermilk or nonfat dry milk solids mixed with water) make a lunch that keeps most people happy. It is the dinners, and especially the desserts, that are the hardest to plan, isn't it?

There are six complete dinner menus here, all averaging about 600 calories per person. Only six menus may seem skimpy to you, but they are merely meant as patterns to point the way to the many fine foods on your market shelves that make calorie watching much easier and tastier today than ever before. You'll find dozens of low-calorie salad dressings, soft drinks, milk ice creams, sugar and cream substitutes and low-calorie canned fruits and preserves. Research over the last few years has improved these foods until they resemble their fattening counterparts so closely that who could say, simply by tasting them, which is which?

If you are too plump and just can't resist rich desserts, this chapter is *especially* for you. Following the dinner menus you'll find recipes for a dozen desserts—such good desserts that no one would guess they are all under 130 calories per serving. Some are even under 100! Compare that with the

600 calories packed into the average piece of apple pie à la mode! Even a half portion of these desserts sneaked at bedtime needn't bother your conscience much. The ingredients are given in quantities to serve six, eight or ten, since all of these yummy creations keep well in the refrigerator for a second round—even a third. More to the point, they are ideal for serving at dessert-and-coffee get-togethers. With one of them as the party fare, you need no longer stick out like a sore thumb, munching away on a piece of fruit while everyone else is reveling in some fabulous concoction.

These recipes have another "plus." They are low in saturated fats, in case your doctor has advised restricting cholesterol. Salt substitutes may be used throughout, too, to make them low-salt, low-cholesterol and low in calories all at the same time.

If you are a diabetic, that's something else again. These recipes aren't sugar free. All of them aren't low in carbohydrates. So play it safe. Your diet is an individual one, and only your doctor can decide what you can and can't eat.

CALORIE WATCHER'S DINNER MENUS

Menu I

Jellied Consommé
Crisp Baked Chicken*
Small Paprika Potato
Spinach with Lemon Wedge
Tomato Salad
Bottled Low-calorie Roquefort or French Dressing
Baked Coconut Custard*
Tea or Coffee
(with sugar and cream substitutes, if desired)

CRISP BAKED CHICKEN

2 chicken parts	⅛ teaspoon salt
3 tablespoons commercial	2 teaspoons sesame seeds
sour cream	Dash paprika
1 tablespoon lemon juice	Chopped parsley
¼ teaspoon crushed	
rosemary leaves	

Heat oven to 375° F. Wash and dry chicken. Blend sour cream, lemon juice, rosemary, salt. Spread chicken with half of the sour cream mixture and arrange it in a shallow baking pan. Bake in preheated oven for 50 minutes or until fork-tender. Brush with the remaining sour cream mixture. Sprinkle with sesame seeds and paprika. Bake 10 minutes longer. Garnish with chopped parsley. Makes 2 servings, each about 220 calories.

BAKED COCONUT CUSTARD

⅔ cup water	½ teaspoon liquid sugar
⅔ cup nonfat dry milk	substitute
solids	¼ teaspoon almond extract
1 egg	Dash salt
2 teaspoons sugar	3 teaspoons flaked coconut

Heat oven to 300° F. Pour the water and dry milk solids into a jar and shake until blended. Beat egg slightly. Add sugar, sugar substitute, almond extract and salt. Stir in blended milk. Pour into 3 greased 6-ounce custard cups. Stir 1 teaspoon of the coconut into each cup. Place in a pan filled with water to within ¾ inch of the top of the custards. Bake 50 minutes, or until set. Makes 3 servings, each about 106 calories.

Menu II

Barbecued Beef Liver*
Tomato Rice*
Lightly Buttered Celery and Carrots
Lettuce and Canned Artichoke Salad
Low-calorie Russian Dressing
Melba Toast
Spiced Fruit Compote*
Tea or Coffee
(with sugar and cream substitutes, if desired)

BARBECUED BEEF LIVER

2 slices beef liver (about ½ pound)
2 tablespoons low-calorie French or Roquefort dressing
1 3-ounce can sliced mushrooms, drained

Brush both sides of the liver with dressing. Place on broiler rack. Broil 5 inches from heat for about 4 minutes. Turn; broil 2 minutes on the other side. Cover with mushrooms and broil 2 minutes longer. Makes 2 servings, each about 175 calories.

TOMATO RICE

¾ cup tomato juice
⅓ cup raw regular white
   rice

⅛ teaspoon salt
½ teaspoon dried parsley
   flakes

Bring tomato juice to a boil in the top of a double boiler over direct heat. Stir in remaining ingredients. Set over boiling water. Cover and cook for 20 to 25 minutes or until moisture is absorbed and rice is tender and fluffy. Makes 2 servings, each about 135 calories.

SPICED FRUIT COMPOTE

1 8-ounce can dietetic-pack
   peach halves
1 8-ounce can dietetic-pack
   pear halves
1 8-ounce can sour red
   cherries packed in water

2 whole cloves
1 stick cinnamon, about 3
   inches long
2 tablespoons brown sugar

Drain canned fruits, reserving juice. Combine juice, cloves, cinnamon and brown sugar in a small saucepan. Bring to a boil. Stir until sugar is dissolved and cook until liquid is reduced to about ¾ cup. Pour hot syrup over the fruit. Let stand 15 minutes. Serve warm. Makes 3 generous servings, each about 90 calories.

If you prefer, serve fruits chilled: Let stand 15 minutes at room temperature. Remove cloves and cinnamon. Chill.

Menu III

Vegetable Juice Cocktail
Broiled Club Steak
Lightly Buttered Frozen Mixed Vegetables
Melba Toast
Cottage Cheese and Asparagus Salad
Bottled Low-calorie Russian Dressing
Peaches in Sherry*
Tea or Coffee
(with sugar and cream substitutes, if desired)

PEACHES IN SHERRY

1 8-ounce can dietetic-pack
  peach halves
1 tablespoon sherry
⅛ teaspoon ground
  cinnamon

Dash ground nutmeg
2 tablespoons toasted
  flaked coconut

Drain peaches, reserving juice. Mix juice, sherry, cinnamon and nutmeg. Pour over peaches and chill. Serve garnished with coconut. Makes 2 servings, each about 59 calories.

Menu IV

Consommé with two Crisp Crackers
Savory Broiled Fillets*
Steamed Rice (about ½ cup each)
Broiled Half Tomato
Hearts of Lettuce   Yoghurt Dressing*
Broiled Grapefruit with Rum*
Tea or Coffee
(with sugar substitute and milk, if desired)

SAVORY BROILED FILLETS

2 fillets of flounder (about   1 teaspoon parsley flakes
    ½ pound each)   ⅛ teaspoon salt
1 tablespoon mayonnaise   Dash pepper
2 teaspoons lemon juice   Dash paprika
1 thinly sliced green
    onion or 1 teaspoon
    grated onion

Heat broiler. Wipe fillets dry with a paper towel. In a small bowl combine mayonnaise, lemon juice, onion, parsley, salt and pepper. Arrange fillets in broiler pan. Spread with mayonnaise mixture. Broil 5 inches from heat for 7 to 8 minutes or until fish flakes easily when tested with a fork. Sprinkle with paprika. Makes 2 servings, each about 175 calories.

YOGHURT DRESSING

1 egg yolk[1]   ¼ teaspoon paprika
¼ teaspoon celery salt   ¾ cup unflavored yoghurt
¼ teaspoon dry mustard   1 tablespoon lemon juice

In a small bowl beat the egg yolk, celery salt, mustard and paprika with a fork until well blended. Gradually beat in yoghurt and lemon juice. Makes about 1 cup of dressing. About 9 calories per tablespoon.

[1] Freeze the egg white, as directed in Chapter Two, unless you plan to use it within a day.

BROILED GRAPEFRUIT WITH RUM

1 large grapefruit, halved
1 tablespoon dark rum²

2 tablespoons low-calorie
   apricot preserves
1 teaspoon melted butter

Cut out the center and remove seeds from each grapefruit half. With a sharp knife cut around each section to loosen it. Sprinkle each half with rum, then spread with preserves. Drizzle with melted butter. Run under the broiler, 5 inches from heat, for about 4 minutes or until the grapefruit is bubbly. Serve hot. Makes 2 servings, each about 115 calories.

² If you prefer, substitute 1 tablespoon of any fruit juice and ⅛ teaspoon rum extract for rum.

Menu V

Tomato Consommé
Salisbury Steak*
Small Parsley Potato
Lightly Buttered Chopped Broccoli with Lemon Wedge
Tossed Green Salad   Low-calorie Cottage Cheese Dressing*
Strawberry Milk Ice Cream
or
Unflavored Yoghurt Topped with a Tablespoon of
Low-calorie Strawberry Preserves
Tea or Coffee
(with sugar and cream substitutes, if desired)

SALISBURY STEAK

½ *pound lean ground*   ¼ *teaspoon salt*
  chuck   *Dash pepper*
2 *tablespoons raw*   1 *tablespoon catsup*
  quick-cooking oats
1 *tablespoon chopped*
  onion

Heat broiler. Combine all ingredients in a bowl. Blend well. Form the mixture into 2 patties about 1 inch thick. Arrange them in broiler pan. Broil 5 inches from heat. For medium-rare, broil 5 minutes on one side, 4 on the other, or broil to desired doneness. Makes 2 servings, each about 300 calories.

LOW-CALORIE COTTAGE CHEESE DRESSING

¼ *cup cream-style cottage*   1 *tablespoon chili sauce*
  cheese   1 *teaspoon chopped parsley*
¼ *cup milk*   ⅛ *teaspoon celery seed*
¼ *teaspoon salt*   *(optional)*
1 *tablespoon lemon*
  juice

Mash cottage cheese well with the back of a wooden spoon. Blend in milk, salt, lemon juice, chili sauce, parsley and celery seed. Makes ½ cup dressing, about 14 calories per tablespoon. Keep in the refrigerator and use within 4 days.

Menu VI

Chilled Tomato Juice
Barbecued Chicken*
Small Serving Steamed Rice (about ½ cup each)
Lightly Buttered Green Beans and Mushrooms
Cottage Cheese-Stuffed Celery   Carrot Sticks
Parker House Roll   Half Pat Butter or Margarine
Orange-Wine Cream*
Tea or Coffee
(with sugar and cream substitutes, if desired)

BARBECUED CHICKEN

2 tablespoons bottled   1 teaspoon chopped chives
  low-calorie French   2 chicken parts
  dressing   Salt and pepper
1 teaspoon lemon juice

Heat broiler. Combine French dressing, lemon juice and chives. Arrange chicken, skin side down, in broiler pan. Brush with half of the dressing mixture. Broil 5 inches from heat for 10 minutes. Turn; brush with the rest of the dressing mixture. Sprinkle with salt and pepper. Continue to broil for 20 minutes or until fork-tender. Makes 2 servings, each about 175 calories.

ORANGE-WINE CREAM

*1½ teaspoons unflavored
    gelatine*
¼ cup dry sherry
1 egg
⅔ cup orange juice
*½ teaspoon grated orange
    rind*

*¾ teaspoon liquid sugar
    substitute*
¼ cup ice water
*¼ cup nonfat dry milk
    solids*
1½ teaspoons lemon juice

Sprinkle gelatine over sherry in the top of a double boiler. Let stand 5 minutes. Place over boiling water until dissolved. Beat the egg. Stir in the orange juice. Gradually add the gelatine mixture. Blend and pour back into the top of the double boiler. Cook over simmering water, stirring occasionally, for 5 minutes or until the mixture is slightly thickened. Stir in the orange rind and sugar substitute. Place the pan with the orange mixture in a bowl of ice cubes and chill, stirring occasionally, until slightly thickened. Combine ice water, dry milk solids and lemon juice in a small bowl. Beat with rotary beater until soft peaks form. Fold whipped milk into the gelatine mixture and pour it into serving dishes. Chill until firm, about 2 hours. Makes 3 servings, each about 107 calories.

A DOZEN MOUTH-WATERING
LOW-CALORIE DESSERTS

LEMON CHEESECAKE

2 tablespoons packaged
    cereal crumbs
1 3¾-ounce package
    lemon-flavored whipped
    dessert mix (such as
    Whip 'n Chill)
1 cup skim-milk cottage
    cheese
½ teaspoon liquid sugar
    substitute

1 envelope low-calorie
    whipped topping mix
    (such as Dream Whip)
Few drops red food
    coloring
¼ cup low-calorie
    strawberry preserves

Lightly butter an 8-inch cake pan—one with a removable
bottom. Dust the bottom and sides of the pan with cereal
crumbs. Prepare the lemon-flavored mix as the package directs, substituting skim milk for the whole milk called for in
the directions. Mash the cottage cheese with a fork. Stir
cottage cheese and sugar substitute into the lemon whip. Prepare whipped topping mix as package directs. Blend it into
the lemon mixture. Pour into the prepared pan. Chill until
firm—at least 3 hours. Add a few drops of red food coloring
to the strawberry preserves. Spread preserves over the top of
the cheesecake. Run a small, sharp knife around the sides
of the pan. Push the cake out of the pan, leaving it on the pan
bottom. Cut in wedges. Makes 8 servings, each about 125
calories.

CHOCOLATE RUM CREAM

*1 4-serving envelope
chocolate-flavored
low-calorie pudding and
pie filling mix*
*⅓ cup nonfat dry milk
solids*
*1 8-ounce can dietetic-pack
pears*

*Water plus juice drained
from pears to make 1⅔
cups liquid*
*1 envelope low-calorie
whipped topping mix*
½ teaspoon rum extract

In a small saucepan combine pudding mix and dry milk solids. Stir until thoroughly blended. Drain and slice pears. Pour juice drained from pears into a 2-cup measure. Add water to make 1⅔ cups liquid. Gradually stir this liquid into the pudding mixture and cook, stirring constantly, over medium heat, until the pudding comes to a boil. Cool to room temperature. Prepare whipped topping mix as package directs. Stir in rum extract.

Fold pears and about ⅔ of the whipped topping into the chocolate pudding. Chill the rest of the topping until serving time. Spoon pudding into 6 dessert dishes or sherbet glasses. Chill. (Pudding thickens as it chills.) Serve topped with dollops of the remaining whipped topping.[8] Make 6 servings, each about 112 calories.

[8] Topping may become too thick upon standing. If so, add 1 or 2 teaspoons cold water and beat with a fork until creamy.

RASPBERRY CREAM SPONGE ROLL

4 eggs

¾ cup sugar

¾ cup sifted cake flour

¾ teaspoon baking
  powder

¼ teaspoon salt

½ teaspoon ground
  cinnamon

1 teaspoon vanilla extract

1 teaspoon confectioners'
  sugar

1 envelope low-calorie
  whipped topping mix

¼ cup low-calorie raspberry
  preserves

Let eggs warm up to room temperature. Heat oven to 375° F. Grease a 15½ × 10½ × 1-inch jelly roll pan. Line it with waxed paper and grease again. Break eggs into a deep bowl. Beat until light and fluffy. Gradually add sugar, beating after each addition. Combine flour, baking powder, salt and cinnamon. Add at one time to the egg mixture. Blend well. Stir in vanilla. Turn batter into prepared pan. Spread it out evenly. Bake in preheated oven for 15 minutes or until the cake springs back when lightly touched in the center. Dust a towel with the confectioners' sugar. Turn cake out onto sugared towel. Quickly remove paper and trim off the crisp edges of the cake. Roll it up in the towel jelly-roll fashion. Cool.

To serve: Prepare whipped topping mix as package directs. Carefully unroll cake. Spread it with the preserves, then with about ⅔ of the whipped topping. Roll up again. Chill for about 15 minutes. Slice and garnish each serving with a dollop of the reserved whipped topping. Makes 10 servings, each about 130 calories.

LEMON CHIFFON GINGER PIE

½ cup finely crushed
   packaged gingersnaps
2 teaspoons melted butter
   or margarine
1 3¾-ounce package
   lemon-flavored whipped
   dessert mix

½ teaspoon powdered
   ginger
2 tablespoons very finely
   chopped crystallized
   ginger

Grease the bottom and sides of an 8-inch pie plate. Combine gingersnap crumbs and melted butter. Set aside 2 tablespoons of the crumbs. Sprinkle the rest over the bottom and sides of the pie plate. Prepare the lemon-flavored mix as package directs, substituting skim milk for the whole milk called for in the directions. Blend in powdered ginger and crystallized ginger. Pour into the prepared pan. Sprinkle reserved crumbs around the edge. Chill until firm, about 2 hours. Makes 6 servings, each about 120 calories.

APRICOT BAVARIAN CREAM

1 package vanilla-flavored
   whipped dessert mix
½ cup low-calorie apricot
   preserves
½ teaspoon mint extract

1 envelope low-calorie
   whipped topping mix
Few sprigs of mint
   (optional)

Whip dessert mix as package directs, substituting ½ cup cold water for the ½ cup cold milk called for in the directions. Stir in preserves and mint extract. Prepare whipped topping mix as package directs. Reserve ½ cup. Fold the rest of the topping into the apricot mixture. Pour it into a 4-cup mold. Chill at least 3 hours. Unmold onto a chilled dessert plate and garnish with remaining whipped topping[4] and mint leaves, if desired. Makes 6 servings, each about 120 calories.

[4] If reserved topping becomes too stiff upon standing, add 1 or 2 teaspoons cold water and beat with a fork until creamy.

CHILLED LEMON SOUFFLÉ WITH FRESH STRAWBERRY SAUCE

2 3¾-ounce packages
  lemon-flavored whipped
  dessert mix
1 envelope low-calorie
  whipped topping mix
2 teaspoons grated lemon
  rind

1 cup hulled, sliced
  strawberries
¼ cup low-calorie
  strawberry preserves
Few drops red food
  coloring

Lightly grease the bottom and sides of a 1½-quart soufflé pan. Make a double-thick aluminum foil collar 4 inches wide and long enough to go around the top of the soufflé pan plus a 1-inch overlap. Arrange the collar around the outside of the pan to form an overlapping rim 1½ inches higher than the edge. Tie it securely in place.

Prepare the lemon-flavored mix as the package directs, substituting skim milk for the whole milk called for. Prepare the topping mix as the package directs. Reserve about ⅔ cup of whipped topping. Fold the rest of it into the lemon whip. Stir in the lemon rind. Pour the mixture into the prepared soufflé pan and chill ½ hour. Then stir the berries into the preserves. Add a few drops red food coloring. Spread over the soufflé and chill for at least 3 more hours.

To serve: Carefully remove the foil collar. Garnish with reserved whipped topping.[5] Makes 10 servings, each about 130 calories.

[5] If topping becomes too stiff upon standing, add 1 to 2 teaspoons cold water. Beat with a fork until creamy.

MARBLE COCONUT BOMBE

1 4-serving envelope
vanilla low-calorie
pudding and pie filling
mix
1 3¾-ounce package
chocolate-flavored
whipped dessert mix

¼ cup low-calorie whipped
topping mix
¼ cup very cold water
2 tablespoons flaked
coconut

Prepare vanilla pudding mix as package directs, using skim milk instead of the whole milk called for. Chill. Beat chocolate dessert mix as package directs, also using skim milk instead of whole milk. Spoon alternate layers of chocolate and vanilla pudding into a 4-cup mold. Using a spatula or knife, cut through the pudding several times to form a marbled effect. Chill at least 4 hours or overnight.

When ready to serve, blend whipped topping mix and cold water in a small bowl. Beat until it is the consistency of whipped cream. Dip the mold quickly into a pan of hot water. Invert pudding onto a chilled serving plate. Spread it with the whipped topping. Sprinkle with coconut. Makes 8 servings, each about 115 calories.

GINGER MELON MOLD

2 envelopes unflavored
  gelatine
¼ cup sugar
½ cup water
½ cup lemon juice
4 teaspoons liquid sugar
  substitute

2 cups low-calorie ginger
  ale
1½ cups honeydew melon
  balls
Mint leaves (optional)

In a small bowl combine gelatine, sugar and water. Set the bowl in a pan of hot water. Stir over low heat until gelatine is all dissolved. Cool slightly. Stir in lemon juice, liquid sugar substitute and ginger ale. Chill until the mixture begins to thicken. Add melon balls and pour into a 5-cup mold. Chill until firm, at least 3 hours. Unmold onto a chilled serving plate and garnish, if desired, with mint leaves. Makes 8 servings, each about 50 calories.

APPLESAUCE COOKIES

1½ cups all-purpose flour
½ teaspoon salt
1 teaspoon ground cinnamon
½ teaspoon ground nutmeg
½ teaspoon ground cloves
1 teaspoon baking powder
½ cup shortening

½ cup brown sugar, packed
½ teaspoon vanilla extract
1 egg
¾ cup canned low-calorie
  applesauce
2 cups Raisin Bran flakes

Heat oven to 375° F. Sift together flour, salt, spices and baking powder. Cream shortening and brown sugar. Stir in vanilla. Beat egg slightly and add to sugar mixture. Add flour mixture and applesauce alternately to egg mixture, blending well after each addition. Fold in cereal flakes. Drop dough by rounded teaspoonfuls, 1 inch apart, onto greased cookie sheets. Bake in preheated oven about 20 minutes or until crisp and lightly browned. Makes 4 dozen cookies, each about 50 calories.

BUTTERSCOTCH REFRIGERATOR COOKIES

1 cup sifted all-purpose
*   flour*
½ teaspoon baking powder
Dash salt
¼ cup butter, margarine
*   or shortening*
2 tablespoons brown sugar

1 envelope (4-serving size)
*   low-calorie butterscotch*
*   pudding and pie filling*
*   mix*
1 egg
¼ teaspoon vanilla extract

Sift flour with baking powder and salt. Cream butter and sugar. Gradually stir in pudding mix and blend well. Add egg and vanilla and beat until mixture is light and fluffy. Gradually add flour mixture, blending well. Place dough on a sheet of waxed paper. Shape it into a roll about 2 inches in diameter. Wrap in waxed paper and chill in the freezer for 30 minutes or in the refrigerator overnight. Heat oven to 375° F. Cut dough into ⅛-inch slices and arrange them on an ungreased cookie sheet. Bake in preheated oven for 8 to 10 minutes or until cookies just begin to brown slightly around the edges. Makes about 2 dozen cookies, each about 43 calories.

PARTY RICE PUDDINGS

3 cups skim milk (or use
  nonfat dry milk solids
  and water to make 3
  cups skim milk)
1 stick cinnamon, 2 inches
  long
¼ cup raw regular white
  rice
¼ cup sugar

¼ cup seedless raisins
1 egg
½ teaspoon liquid sugar
  substitute
⅛ teaspoon salt
1 teaspoon vanilla extract
1 envelope low-calorie
  whipped topping mix

Combine milk, cinnamon, rice and sugar in the top of a double boiler. Cook over boiling water for 45 minutes. Remove cinnamon. Add raisins and cook 10 minutes longer. Beat egg slightly. Stir egg, sugar substitute, salt and vanilla into rice mixture. Cook 2 minutes longer. Chill. Whip dessert topping mix as package directs. Fold half into the rice pudding. Spoon pudding into dessert dishes or parfait glasses. Top with remaining whipped topping. Makes 8 servings, each about 125 calories.

COFFEE MOUSSE

½ cup cold water
1 envelope unflavored
  gelatine
1 cup nonfat dry milk
  solids
¾ cup water
2 tablespoons instant coffee
  powder

2 tablespoons sugar
1 teaspoon liquid sugar
  substitute
¼ teaspoon almond extract
½ cup ice water
¼ cup low-calorie whipped
  topping mix
¼ cup cold water

Measure the ½ cup cold water into a small saucepan. Sprinkle gelatine over it. Set pan over low heat and stir until gelatine is dissolved. Remove from heat. Dissolve half of the dry milk solids in the ¾ cup water. Add to dissolved gelatine along with coffee, sugar, sugar substitute and almond extract. Blend well. Chill until it is the consistency of unbeaten egg whites. Meanwhile, with a rotary beater or electric mixer beat the remaining ½ cup of dry milk solids with the ice water until stiff peaks form when beater is raised. Beat the whipped milk into the gelatine mixture. Spoon it into 6 sherbet dishes. Chill.

When ready to serve, combine the topping mix and ¼ cup cold water in a small bowl. Beat until it is the consistency of whipped cream. Garnish puddings with whipped topping. Makes 6 servings, each about 130 calories.

Chapter Nine

ESPECIALLY FOR MEN

Where did you ever get the idea (if you have it) that cooking isn't for men? Aren't the famous chefs almost all men? Now that you have plenty of time to develop new hobbies, who knows? You may become a second Escoffier!

Think of the money you can save. Think of the friends you are going to have knocking themselves out to get ahead of each other for one of your dinner invitations! People will be inviting you over for dinner, not only because you are the sought-after extra man, but because they hope for a return invitation. You'll be the most popular man in the neighborhood.

Now before you say, "This isn't for me. I can't cook," just think what it would cost you to "pay off" a few dinner obligations at a good restaurant or hotel dining room. You won't want to think about it long—not unless you are richer than most. For less than a third of the cost of the average such evening, you, by yourself, can prepare any one of the following meals, entertain old friends, make new ones and enjoy the role of host. Though at first glance they may look pretty gourmet for inexperienced chefs, each recipe, with its step-by-step instructions, is easy to prepare. Supposing you concentrate on one of the menus. Be famous for your curry, or your shish kebobs or whichever appeals to you most. Then go on to other culinary conquests. When it comes to setting the table, what man can be expected to do that? Correctly, anyway? Flatter one of your feminine guests into doing it for you. Just say, "You do everything so easily, I'm counting on you to set the table while I'm fixing the drinks."

Do your shopping a day ahead of time. With each of the

five menus that follow there is a list of everything you will need. You may have plenty of coffee, tea and butter, but these items, too, are listed as reminders just in case you are running low. The only thing for you to plan yourself is the predinner sociable liquids.

Menu I

Cocktails or Tomato Juice in the Living Room
Nibblers
(such as Corn Chips, Crackers, Cheese)
Festive Lamb Shish Kebobs*
Fried Rice*
Tossed Green Salad
Heated Packaged Rolls   Butter or Margarine
Crème de Menthe Sundae*
Frozen Brownies
Tea or Coffee

Shopping List for Menu I

Ingredients for predinner drinks and snacks
1½ pounds lean boneless lamb, cut in 1½-inch cubes
2 lemons (only 1 if you are serving coffee; the second
  lemon is for wedges if you serve tea)
1 bud garlic
Small bottle olive oil
Dried parsley flakes
2 medium-sized onions
2 firm, medium-sized tomatoes
1 medium-sized green pepper
½ pound fairly large mushrooms
White rice (regular or "converted")—you'll need 1 cup,
  in case you already have some on hand

1 13¾-ounce can chicken broth
1 head lettuce
1 small head romaine or escarole
1 small cucumber (optional)
1 bottle Italian-style dressing
1 package rolls
Butter or margarine
1 pint vanilla ice cream
Small bottle crème de menthe
1 13-ounce package frozen brownies
Coffee or tea
Sugar for beverage
Light cream, if serving coffee

Order of Preparation for Menu I

DAY AHEAD OF TIME

· Do your food shopping.
· Prepare marinade for Festive Lamb Shish Kebobs.* Pour it over the lamb as the recipe directs. Refrigerate overnight.
· Wash salad greens (lettuce and romaine). Put in the refrigerator until needed—cucumber, too, if you bought one.

ON THE DAY OF YOUR DINNER PARTY

· Several hours ahead of time tear salad greens into bite-sized pieces. Peel and slice cucumber. Arrange greens and cucumber in a salad bowl and chill until needed. Serve tossed with Italian dressing.
· Make Fried Rice.* This can be done well ahead of time to save last-minute confusion. Pour it into an ovenware casserole; cover and heat in the oven the last 30 minutes with the shish kebobs. Or reheat it in the top of a double boiler over boiling water. This will take about 20 minutes.

• An hour ahead of time "thread" lamb and vegetables onto skewers as recipe directs. Bake as directed.

LAST-MINUTE ACTIVITIES

• Heat rolls along with shish kebobs the last ten minutes before serving dinner.

• Heat water for tea. Or make coffee.

FESTIVE LAMB SHISH KEBOBS

1½ pounds boned leg of lamb, cut in 1½-inch pieces

1 clove garlic, peeled and chopped

1 teaspoon salt

¼ teaspoon pepper

⅓ cup olive oil

½ teaspoon powdered thyme

Juice of 1 lemon (about 3 tablespoons)

1 green pepper, cut in quarters and seeds removed

2 medium-sized tomatoes, cut in half

8 large mushrooms (about ½ pound)

Trim off any excess fat from lamb. Combine garlic, salt, pepper, olive oil, thyme and lemon juice. Arrange lamb in a shallow pan and pour olive oil marinade over it, turning to coat all pieces well. Let stand at least 4 hours or overnight in the refrigerator. Turn meat several times so that it is well seasoned with the marinade.

Several hours before serving time "thread" the chunks of lamb onto 2 long skewers. Let stand at room temperature.

One hour before serving time heat oven to 375° F. Arrange skewers with meat in a shallow roasting pan. Pour the marinade over the lamb. Bake in preheated oven for 30 minutes. Turn meat to brown on the other side. Thread vegetables onto 2 long skewers and place the skewers of vegetables in the pan beside the lamb. Continue to bake for 20 to 25 minutes, or until vegetables and lamb are tender, basting occasionally with the marinade in the pan.

To serve: Remove lamb and vegetables to a heated platter. Makes 4 generous servings.

Note: Lamb and vegetables may be broiled instead of roasted, but, if so, they take more last-minute watching and turning. Baked shish kebobs make it easier to be a host as well as a chef.

FRIED RICE

3 tablespoons butter or
   margarine
1 cup raw white rice
¼ cup finely chopped
   onion

1 13¾-ounce can chicken
   broth plus water to
   make 2½ cups liquid
1 teaspoon salt
¼ teaspoon pepper
1 tablespoon dried parsley
   flakes

Heat butter in a large saucepan with tight-fitting cover. Add rice and stir it with a wooden spoon over low heat until it is lightly browned. Stir in onion and cook, stirring, until onion is slightly browned, about 1 minute. Remove saucepan with rice from heat and let cool 5 minutes. Stir in chicken broth and water, salt, pepper and parsley. Cover tightly and cook over low heat for 20 to 25 minutes, or until rice is tender and liquid absorbed. Makes 4 to 6 servings.

CRÈME DE MENTHE SUNDAE

1 pint vanilla ice cream

½ cup green crème de
   menthe

Spoon ice cream into 4 dessert dishes. Pour about 2 tablespoons crème de menthe over each. Serve at once. Makes 4 servings.

Menu II

Cocktails and Snacks as in Menu I
Roast Loin of Pork with Pan-Roasted Potatoes*
Spiced Crab Apples
Buttered Frozen Peas and Onions
Celery Hearts   Olives
Heated Packaged Rolls   Butter or Margarine
Frozen Ice Cream Cake Roll
Tea or Coffee

Shopping List for Menu II

Your choice for predinner hospitality
1 6-rib pork loin roast
1 jar spiced crab apples
6 small potatoes
2 10-ounce packages frozen peas and onions
1 bunch celery
1 jar stuffed olives
1 package rolls
Butter or margarine
1 12-ounce frozen ice cream roll (ice cream and cake)
Tea or coffee
Lemon, if serving tea
Cream, if serving coffee
Sugar

Order of Preparation

DAY AHEAD OF TIME

· Do the food shopping.

ON THE DAY OF YOUR DINNER PARTY, WELL AHEAD OF
TIME

• Arrange crab apples in a serving dish. Refrigerate.
• Clean celery and arrange it and the olives in a serving
dish. Cover with plastic wrap, foil or wax paper. Refrigerate.
• Peel potatoes. Put them in a bowl of cold water.

ABOUT TWO HOURS BEFORE DINNERTIME

• Heat the oven for the pork roast. Roast pork and potatoes, following the directions in the recipe for Roast Loin
of Pork with Pan-Roasted Potatoes.*

LAST-MINUTE ACTIVITIES

• Heat rolls in the oven with the pork the last 10 minutes.
• Heat water for tea. Or make coffee.

ROAST LOIN OF PORK WITH PAN-ROASTED POTATOES

1 6-rib pork loin roast
5 to 6 peeled small potatoes (about 1½ pounds)
Salt

Heat oven to 350° F. Place pork, fat side up, in a shallow
roasting pan. Roast in preheated oven for ½ hour. Blot
potatoes dry with a paper towel. Arrange them in the pan
around the roast. Sprinkle with salt. Continue to bake for
about 1 hour and 15 minutes longer, turning the potatoes
about every 20 minutes and basting them with fat in the pan.
Pork should be well done—not the least bit pink when you
serve it. When it has roasted 1 hour and 45 minutes, insert a
knife deep into the center. If meat is gray, it is done. If not,
continue to roast another 10 to 15 minutes or until all

traces of pink disappear. Potatoes and meat will be done at approximately the same time. If potatoes do not seem quite tender, remove the pork to a heated serving platter. Turn oven to 425° F. Potatoes will be tender in a very few minutes. Makes 4 servings with seconds for 2, or with leftovers for your dinner tomorrow.

Menu III

Cocktails and Snacks as in Menu I
Chicken Breasts Amandine*
Cranberry Sauce
Baked Idaho Potatoes
Buttered Frozen Green Beans
Sliced Tomato Salad Cruet of Bottled Dressing
—Your Choice
Garlic French Bread*
Cherries Jubilee* or Ice Cream and Packaged Cookies
Tea or Coffee

Shopping List for Menu III

Choice of drinks and snacks
3 double chicken breasts, split and boned
1 bag (at least ⅓ cup) blanched slivered almonds
Paprika
1 bud garlic
½ pint commercial sour cream
Parsley flakes
1 1-pound can whole cranberry sauce
6 medium-sized potatoes
1 1-pound plastic bag frozen green beans
1 ripe large tomato

Lettuce or water cress
Bottled salad dressing—your choice
1 small loaf French bread
Butter or margarine
1 jar grated Parmesan cheese
1 quart vanilla ice cream
1 1-pound-1-ounce can pitted Bing cherries
1 orange
Cornstarch (you'll need only 2 teaspoons)
Sugar
Ground cinnamon
About ¼ cup brandy or cognac
Coffee or tea
Lemon for tea
Cream for coffee

Order of Preparation

DAY AHEAD OF TIME

• Shop for all food.

MORNING OF YOUR DINNER PARTY

• Prepare Garlic French Bread* to be ready to heat.
• Scrub potatoes ready to bake.
• Make sauce for Cherries Jubilee.* Keep it at room temperature, ready to reheat and ignite at dessert time.
• Arrange lettuce leaves or water cress and tomato slices on chilled salad plates. Place salads in the refrigerator until dinnertime.

LATE AFTERNOON BEFORE THE PARTY

• About 1½ hours before dinner start to prepare Chicken Breasts Amandine.* Bake as recipe directs.

· Bake potatoes in the same oven with the chicken. Chicken and potatoes will be done at approximately the same time.

LAST-MINUTE ACTIVITIES

· Cook beans in boiling salted water to cover. They will take about 20 minutes.

· Heat Garlic French Bread* in the oven with the chicken 10 minutes before dinner.

· Heat water for tea, or make coffee.

CHICKEN BREASTS AMANDINE

3 *double chicken breasts, split apart and boned*	1 *teaspoon instant minced onion*
2 *tablespoons flour*	½ *cup commercial sour cream*
½ *teaspoon salt*	
½ *teaspoon paprika*	⅓ *cup slivered blanched almonds*
3 *tablespoons butter or margarine*	1 *teaspoon parsley flakes*

Have butcher bone chicken breasts. Wash them and wipe them dry with paper towels. In a brown paper bag combine flour, salt and paprika. Shake chicken pieces, a few at a time, in the flour mixture. Heat butter in a skillet. Brown chicken in hot butter, turning to brown lightly on both sides. Remove chicken to a shallow baking pan. (If you wish, this much can be done in the morning. If so, place the pan of chicken in the refrigerator until about 1 hour before serving time.)

Heat oven to 400° F. Bake chicken for 30 minutes. Stir onion into sour cream. Spread chicken with the sour cream mixture and continue to bake for 20 minutes. Sprinkle with almonds. Bake 10 minutes longer. Arrange chicken on a serving platter and sprinkle with parsley. Makes 6 servings.

GARLIC FRENCH BREAD

⅓ cup soft butter or
  margarine
1 small clove garlic, sliced
2 tablespoons grated
  Parmesan cheese

1 small loaf French bread
  (about 10 inches long)

In a small bowl combine the butter, garlic and half of the cheese. Let stand 1 hour. Remove garlic. Make diagonal cuts in the bread at 1½-inch intervals from the top almost to the bottom crust. Place the bread on a sheet of foil. Spread the garlic butter between bread slices and over the top. Sprinkle with the remaining cheese. Place bread in the oven with the chicken and potatoes for the last 10 minutes of baking time. Makes 6 servings.

CHERRIES JUBILEE

2 teaspoons cornstarch
⅓ cup sugar
Dash ground cinnamon
1 1-pound-1-ounce can
  pitted Bing cherries
1 teaspoon grated orange
  rind

¼ cup orange juice
3 tablespoons brandy or
  cognac
1 quart vanilla ice cream

Measure cornstarch and sugar into a small saucepan. Add cinnamon and blend the mixture well. Blend in about ½ cup of the cherry juice. Add the remaining cherry juice, cherries, orange rind and orange juice. Bring mixture to a boil over medium heat, stirring constantly. Boil about ½ minute or until the sauce is shiny and slightly thickened.

If sauce is made ahead of time, let it stand at room temperature and warm it again slightly when ready to serve dessert. Warm brandy slightly, too, by pouring it into a small saucepan and heating it ever so slightly over low heat. Spoon ice cream into a serving bowl. Pour warm cherry sauce over it and pour the warm brandy over all. Ignite with a taper or long kitchen match. To impress your guests with the dramatic effect, turn off the lights until the flame dies down. Spoon into individual dessert dishes. Makes 6 servings.

Menu IV

Cocktails and Snacks as in Menu I
Indonesian Chicken Curry*
Curry Trimmings
(Chutney   Shredded Coconut   Chopped Onion
Roasted Peanuts   Seedless Raisins)
Steamed Rice
Celery Hearts   Melba Toast
Canned Mandarin Orange Sections
Packaged Cookies
Tea

Shopping List for Menu IV

Your choice of drinks and snacks
1 4-pound stewing chicken
1 bunch celery
Ground cumin
Ground coriander
Ground turmeric
Ground ginger
Ground cloves

Dry mustard
Cayenne
1 jar instant minced onion
Butter or margarine
Flour (you'll need 2 tablespoons)
2 large onions
1 bottle chutney
1 can shredded coconut
Seedless raisins (about ⅓ cup) or roasted peanuts
Regular white rice
1 package melba toast
2 11-ounce cans mandarin orange sections
Packaged cookies
Tea
Sugar and lemon for tea

Order of Preparation

DAY AHEAD OF TIME

· Do the food shopping
· Cook the chicken as recipe for Indonesian Chicken Curry* directs. Remove it from the chicken broth. Let it cool; then pick the meat from the bones. Refrigerate both chicken and broth.

AFTERNOON BEFORE YOUR DINNER PARTY

· Make the curried chicken, following recipe directions.
· Prepare small serving bowls of three or four curry trimmings, ready to be passed at the table. Set the bowls on a large serving plate so that all can be passed at once.
· Wash celery hearts (you will have used the tops in the curry). Arrange them in a serving dish. Refrigerate.
· Arrange melba toast on a plate or in a breadbasket.

· Empty orange sections into a bowl. Chill until dessert time. (Then spoon them into individual dessert dishes.)

· Arrange cookies on a plate.

LAST-HALF-HOUR ACTIVITIES

· Cook rice, following instructions on the package label.
· Reheat curry, following recipe directions.
· Heat water for tea.

You may wonder why there is no mention of curry powder in the shopping list or in the recipe which follows. Actually, curry isn't a spice. Most of us use the patented blends we find on the market shelves. Such blends are a combination of any number of spices. There is no one-and-only formula, so blends vary. In Indonesia, India and other countries where curries are the staple food, everyone takes a bit of this and that spice and makes a curry blend to suit himself.

Few of your guests, no matter how well they cook, will have made their own "from scratch" curry. So astonish them with your ability to concoct an authentic Indonesian Chicken Curry.* It isn't a bit hard to do.

INDONESIAN CHICKEN CURRY

1 4-pound stewing chicken	*⅛ teaspoon ground cloves*
Tops from 1 bunch celery	*¼ teaspoon dry mustard*
3 cups boiling water	*1 teaspoon salt*
2 teaspoons salt	*¼ teaspoon pepper*
2 teaspoons ground	*3 tablespoons butter or*
coriander	*margarine*
2 teaspoons ground	*2½ cups chicken stock*
turmeric	*2 teaspoons instant minced*
1 teaspoon ground cumin	*onion*
½ teaspoon ground ginger	*2 tablespoons flour*
½ teaspoon cayenne	

Day ahead of time combine chicken, celery tops, boiling water and the 2 teaspoons salt in a Dutch oven or large kettle. Cover and simmer for 1 hour and 15 minutes, or until chicken is very tender. Remove chicken from broth and let cool until it can be handled easily. Strain broth and set it aside. Pick the meat from the bones, leaving it in as large pieces as possible. Refrigerate both chicken and broth until ready to use it in your curry.

Several hours ahead of your dinner party, blend together in a small bowl the coriander, turmeric, cumin, ginger, cayenne, cloves, mustard and remaining 1 teaspoon of salt. Add pepper. Melt butter in a large saucepan. Turn heat *very* low. Stir in blended spices and cook, stirring constantly, for 5 minutes. Keep heat low enough so that the mixture barely bubbles. Blend in 1½ cups of the chicken broth and the instant onion. Add chicken pieces. Cover the pan and cook over low heat for 2 to 3 minutes. Stir a few tablespoons of the remaining cup of chicken broth into the flour, making a smooth paste. Add all of the remaining broth to the flour mixture. Then stir it into the hot curry. Cook, stirring, until the mixture is thickened and bubbling hot. Makes 6 servings.

If making your curry midafternoon before your dinner party, reheat it in the top of a double boiler over boiling water. This will take about 20 minutes. Or reheat it over direct heat turned very low, stirring until steaming hot—about 5 minutes.

Menu V

Cocktails and Snacks as in Menu I
Jelly-Glazed Ham Steak*
Baked Sweet Potatoes
Buttered Frozen Mixed Vegetables
Mustard Pickles
Heated Packaged Rolls Butter or Margarine
Assorted Cheese with Crackers
Bowl of Grapes and Pears
Tea or Coffee

Shopping List for Menu V

Cocktail ingredients and snacks—your choice
1 slice ready-to-eat ham, about 1 inch thick (approximately
    1¼ pounds)
1 jar currant jelly (if you keep it on hand, be sure you
    still have ⅓ cup)
Jar of prepared mustard
4 medium-sized sweet potatoes
2 ten-ounce packages buttered frozen mixed vegetables
1 jar cucumber pickles
1 package rolls
Butter or margarine
Crisp crackers (at least 1 dozen more than needed for
    predinner snacks)
1 box assorted, individually wrapped cheese wedges
1 bunch grapes
2 to 3 ripe pears
Tea or coffee
1 lemon (for wedges, if serving tea)
Cream (if serving coffee)
Sugar

Order of Preparation

DAY AHEAD OF TIME

• Do all food shopping.

MIDAFTERNOON BEFORE YOUR DINNER PARTY

• Wash pears and grapes. Arrange fruit and cheese wedges on a serving plate. Refrigerate until 1 hour before dinner.
• Arrange crackers on a plate, ready to serve with fruit and cheese.
• Empty cucumber pickles into a little serving bowl. Chill until dinnertime.
• Wash sweet potatoes. Prick the skin with a fork so that steam will escape during the baking and potatoes won't burst open.

ONE HOUR BEFORE SERVING TIME

• Heat oven to 400° F. Start baking sweet potatoes.
• Prepare Jelly-Glazed Ham Steak* so that it is ready to put in the oven, along with the potatoes, 20 minutes before dinner.
• Remove fruit and cheese from the refrigerator. They are best served at room temperature.

LAST-MINUTE THINGS

• Cook vegetables in boiling salted water—enough to cover them. This will take about 15 minutes.
• Heat rolls in the oven with the potatoes and ham 10 minutes before dinner.
• Heat water for tea, or make coffee.

JELLY-GLAZED HAM STEAK

1 slice (about 1¼ pounds) ready-to-eat ham, about 1 inch
  thick
2 teaspoons prepared mustard
⅓ cup currant jelly

Heat oven to 400° F. Arrange ham slice in a shallow
baking pan. Blend together mustard and jelly. Spread the
mixture over the ham. Bake in preheated oven for 20 minutes
or until sizzling hot. Makes 4 servings.

Chapter Ten

FROM FAMOUS BELOVED AMERICANS

From many and varied walks of life, these famous beloved Americans send their favorite menus and recipes to you, their contemporaries. All above the conventional retirement age, most of these prominent citizens are busy as ever, some even busier.

Sent from Gettysburg, Pennsylvania, this menu, of course, is from Mrs. Dwight David Eisenhower, whose famous husband, former General of the United States Army and our thirty-fourth President looks forward to meals like this. The cookie jar filled with these sugar cookies doesn't stay filled long—certainly not when there are visiting Eisenhower grandchildren.

Mrs. Eisenhower's Menu

Baked Meat Loaf with Brown Gravy
Buttered String Beans Almondise*
Braised Okra or Spinach Soufflé
Strawberry Gelatin Dessert
Mrs. Eisenhower's Sugar Cookies*
Tea

BUTTERED STRING BEANS ALMONDISE

2 pounds green beans,
    washed, trimmed and
    French-cut
2 tablespoons butter or
    margarine

⅓ cup shredded blanched
    almonds
Salt and pepper

Wash beans and remove stem ends and tips. French-cut beans (cut in lengthwise strips). Cook until tender in boiling salted water to cover, about 15 to 20 minutes. Drain. Melt butter; stir in almonds and pour over beans. Season to taste with salt and pepper. Makes 6 servings.

MRS. EISENHOWER'S SUGAR COOKIES

1½ cups all-purpose flour
1 teaspoon baking powder
½ teaspoon salt
½ cup butter or margarine
1 cup sugar

2 egg yolks
1 teaspoon vanilla extract
1 tablespoon light cream
About 2 tablespoons sugar

Sift together flour, baking powder and salt. Cream butter and add the 1 cup sugar slowly, beating after each addition until the mixture is fluffy. Beat the egg yolks well. Stir them, together with the vanilla, into the creamed butter and sugar. Add the dry ingredients alternately with the cream. Form dough into a ball and chill 1 hour. Heat oven to 375° F. Roll out dough on a lightly floured surface to ⅛-inch thickness. Cut in any desired shapes. Arrange cookies on cookie sheets. Sprinkle them with the remaining sugar. Bake in preheated oven for 10 minutes or until lightly browned. Makes 4½ to 6 dozen, depending upon the size of the cutters used.

Mrs. Joseph P. Kennedy, mother of President John F. Kennedy, took time out from a Hyannis Port vacation to send her recipe for Soft Custard.* It came with the comment: "This sauce is a tasty and nutritious one to serve with stewed fruits or puddings."

Mrs. Kennedy's Luncheon Menu for Two

Cup of Vegetable Soup
Chicken and Avocado Salad
Tiny Bread-and-Butter Sandwiches
Stewed Mixed Dried Fruits
with
Mrs. Kennedy's Soft Custard*
Tea

MRS. KENNEDY'S SOFT CUSTARD

2 cups milk   *Pinch salt*
6 egg yolks, slightly beaten   *1 teaspoon vanilla extract*
½ cup sugar

Heat milk in a saucepan until small bubbles form around the edge of the pan. Pour it over the combined beaten egg yolks, sugar and salt. Blend well and cook the mixture in the top of a double boiler over simmering water, stirring constantly, until the custard coats a metal spoon. (Do not let the water in the bottom of the double boiler boil.) Stir in vanilla and chill. Makes about 1 pint of custard sauce.

Marian Anderson, the beloved contralto, known to her family and close friends as Mrs. Orpheus H. Fisher, sends this unusual and tasty recipe for Glorified Rice* from Marianna Farm, the Connecticut home of the Fishers. "Sometimes," she says, "we enjoy the rice with chicken as a part of the main course. But it is equally good as dessert for Sunday supper."

Marian Anderson's Menu

Cranberry Juice Cocktail
Baked Chicken Breasts with Herbs*
Glorified Rice*
Buttered Snap Beans
Crisp Celery Hearts
Fruit Sherbet
Tea   Milk

BAKED CHICKEN BREASTS WITH HERBS

2 *small chicken breasts,* *split*	¼ *teaspoon powdered thyme*
2 *tablespoons flour*	1 *teaspoon lemon juice* *(optional)*
½ *teaspoon salt*	2 *tablespoons melted butter* *or margarine*
Dash pepper	
½ *teaspoon dried rosemary* *leaves*	*Paprika*

Heat oven to 350° F. Wash chicken breasts and wipe them dry with paper towels. Combine flour, salt, pepper, rosemary and thyme in a brown paper bag. Shake chicken pieces in the flour mixture, coating each piece well. Arrange the chicken in a shallow baking pan. Sprinkle with the lemon juice and spoon the melted butter over it. Bake chicken, uncovered, for 45 minutes. Baste with drippings in the pan and continue to bake another 10 to 15 minutes or until very tender and nicely browned. Serve sprinkled with paprika. Makes 2 generous servings.

MARIAN ANDERSON'S GLORIFIED RICE

1 cup cooked rice
1 teaspoon sugar
1 tablespoon butter or
margarine
½ cup seeded or seedless
raisins

½ cup chopped pecans,
walnuts or blanched
almonds[1]

Combine all ingredients in the top of a double boiler. Set over boiling water until piping hot. Makes 2 generous servings.

[1] If using almonds, melt the butter in a saucepan. Add the slivered blanched almonds and stir over low heat until the almonds are golden brown. Blend the nuts and butter into the remaining ingredients and heat as above.

Harry Golden, editor and publisher of the *Carolina Israelite* and author of *Only in America, You're Entitle', Ess, Ess Mein Kindt* and many other dog-eared family favorites, sends his recipe for Holishkas (Stuffed Cabbage).*

Harry Golden's Menu

Holishkas (Stuffed Cabbage)*
Rye Bread
A Bowl of Fresh Grapes and Honey-Ripe Pears
Your Favorite Beverage

HARRY GOLDEN'S HOLISHKAS (STUFFED CABBAGE)

*12 to 14 large cabbage
  leaves
2 pounds ground lean beef
1 cup cooked rice
1½ teaspoons salt
¼ teaspoon pepper
1 6-ounce can tomato paste
1 8-ounce can tomato sauce
1 medium-sized onion,
  chopped*

*½ cup vinegar
2½ cups water
⅓ cup sugar
1 cup seedless raisins
16 to 18 gingersnaps, finely
  crushed (about ⅔ cup
  crumbs)*

Pour boiling water over cabbage leaves. Let stand about 3 minutes or until the leaves are no longer brittle. Drain. In a bowl combine beef, rice, salt and pepper. Mix well. Roll up a portion of the meat mixture in each cabbage leaf, turning under the edges of the cabbage to hold in the stuffing. Combine tomato paste and the rest of the ingredients in a heavy skillet with a tight-fitting cover or in a Dutch oven. Stir the mixture to blend well. Add the cabbage rolls. Baste them with the sauce. Cover and cook over *very* low heat for about 25 to 30 minutes, or until the sauce is thick and the cabbage rolls tender and beginning to brown. Makes 6 to 8 servings.

Here is the favorite recipe of Mrs. Earl Warren, wife of our Chief Justice of the Supreme Court. Of Swedish origin, Bryle' Pudding* combines simplicity with elegance, making it the suitable dessert for many a festive occasion.

MRS. EARL WARREN'S BRYLE' PUDDING

COATING FOR THE PAN

1 cup sugar
½ cup boiling water

CUSTARD

1 quart milk
2 tablespoons sugar
1 tablespoon flour
4 eggs

¼ teaspoon almond extract
8 slivered blanched almonds
or about 1 tablespoon
chopped walnuts

Prepare the pan first. Melt the 1 cup of sugar in a frying pan over very low heat, stirring it constantly with a wooden spoon. *Slowly,* a few drops at a time, add the boiling water. The mixture should look quite brown and frothy. Pour it into a large, deep baking dish or mold. (Mrs. Warren prefers one about 9 inches deep.) Lacking the proper mold, use a 1½-to-2-quart deep bowl. Turn the mold around and around until all sides are completely coated with the burnt sugar mixture. The mixture thickens as it cools and the mold should be evenly coated. This step cannot be hurried. Set the coated bowl, mold or pan aside until needed.

CUSTARD

Pour the 1 quart of milk into the same skillet in which the sugar melted in order to absorb any remaining burnt sugar. Heat it slowly until small bubbles form around the edge of the pan. Cool to lukewarm. Heat oven to 350° F. In a large bowl blend sugar and flour. Add eggs and beat the mixture well. Gradually beat in the lukewarm milk. Stir in the almond extract. Pour into prepared pan. Place it in a large, deep pan. Fill pan with hot water to 1 inch of the top of the custard. Bake in preheated oven for 60 to 70 minutes or until a knife inserted in the center comes out clean. Cool the pudding before unmolding it. With a small pointed knife loosen the top edge from the sides of the pan. Unmold onto a deep-sided serving dish, because the sauce runs down the sides of the pudding and might spill over a flat plate. Garnish with the slivered almonds or chopped walnuts. Makes 6 to 8 servings. This custard can also be made in 8 individual 6-ounce molds or custard cups.

Mr. Frank B. Durkee of Sacramento, California and his wife Wanda need no introduction to Californians. An attorney active in the development of his great state, appointed in 1951 to the position of Director of Public Works for the State of California, and today vice-chairman of Urban Renewal for Sacramento, Frank B. Durkee keeps young with many demanding responsibilities. Entertaining is casual at "Humbug," the Durkee's hideaway retreat, where Mrs. Durkee's Tamale Pie,* which almost cooks by itself, makes being a busy hostess easy.

Mrs. Durkee's Menu

Tamale Pie*
Coleslaw   Beet Pickles
Broiled Angel Food or Sponge Cake Slices*
Coffee

MRS. DURKEE'S TAMALE PIE

The original recipe given in quantities to serve 8 has been adapted to serve 4. For a potluck main dish to serve 8 double the recipe as given below and bake it in 2 1½-quart casseroles or 1 3-quart casserole.

1½ tablespoons vegetable oil	*1 tablespoon chili powder*
1 medium-sized onion,	*¾ cup pitted ripe olives,*
thinly sliced	*drained*
1 pound ground lean chuck	*3 cups cold water*
1 8-ounce can tomato sauce	*1 cup white corn meal²*
1 8-ounce can cream-style	*1 teaspoon salt*
corn	*1½ teaspoons butter or*
1 teaspoon salt	*margarine*
½ teaspoon pepper	

Heat oil in a large, heavy skillet. Add onion and cook over low heat, stirring often, until the onion slices just begin to brown. Remove them and set aside. In the same skillet in which the onions cooked, cook beef over medium heat, breaking it up with a fork as it cooks, and stirring often until lightly browned. Stir in reserved onions, tomato sauce, corn, the 1 teaspoon salt, pepper and chili powder. Cover and cook over low heat for 20 minutes, stirring frequently. Stir in olives.

While meat sauce is cooking, measure the cold water into the top of a double boiler. Place it over direct heat. Turn heat to medium. Gradually stir in the corn meal. Add the remaining teaspoon of salt and cook, stirring constantly, until the mush is thick and beginning to bubble. Set over boiling water. Cover and cook for 30 minutes. Heat oven to 350° F. Line the bottom of a 1½-quart casserole with about ⅔ of the corn meal. Pour in the meat sauce. Dot the surface with small spoonfuls of the remaining mush. Dot mush with butter. Bake, uncovered, in preheated oven for 1 hour. Makes 4 servings.

² Yellow corn meal may be used, if you prefer. Follow directions given on the package label for cooking it.

BROILED ANGEL FOOD OR SPONGE CAKE SLICES

*4 slices homemade or
bakery angel food or
sponge cake, cut ¾- to
1-inch thick*
*1 tablespoon melted butter
or margarine*

*4 well-drained slices of
canned pineapple*
¼ cup brown sugar, packed
*4 teaspoons butter or
margarine*
*Whipped cream or vanilla
ice cream*

Arrange cake slices on a cookie sheet. Spread them lightly with the melted butter. Top each cake slice with one of pineapple. Sprinkle with the brown sugar and dot with butter. Run under the broiler until sugar and butter are melted and the topping lightly browned. Serve topped with whipped cream or ice cream. Makes 4 servings.

The two recipes which follow are favorites of two well-known and beloved clergymen, both internationally known not only as pastors to New York parishes, but as authors of dozens of books and leaders in many areas of church concern.

Mrs. Sockman, wife of Dr. Ralph W. Sockman, minister emeritus of the lovely Park Avenue Christ Church Methodist, New York City, wrote: "Our household enjoys the enclosed recipe for Shrimp and Cheese Casserole,* which I am happy to share with you." Mrs. Peale, wife of Dr. Norman Vincent Peale, pastor, New York's Marble Collegiate Church on lower Fifth Avenue, wrote: "We always enjoy this Onion-Beef-Macaroni Casserole.* It is easy to prepare and economical too. Make it ahead of time, if you wish, and freeze it until you need it. Then just reheat."

Not just stand-bys for family enjoyment, these recipes are the very thing to carry along to a "covered-dish" get-together.

MRS. SOCKMAN'S SHRIMP AND CHEESE CASSEROLE

6 slices white bread
½ pound Old English cheese
1 pound cooked shrimp,
  shelled and deveined
¼ cup melted butter or
  margarine

3 eggs
½ teaspoon dry mustard
½ teaspoon salt
2 cups milk

Break bread into pieces about the size of a quarter. Break cheese into bite-size pieces or cut it in ½-inch cubes. Arrange shrimp, bread and cheese in several layers in a greased 1½- to 2-quart casserole. Pour melted butter over the mixture. Beat the eggs and blend in mustard and salt. Stir in milk and pour the mixture over the ingredients in the casserole. Cover and let stand in the refrigerator at least 3 hours—preferably overnight.

Heat oven to 350° F. Bake the casserole, covered, in preheated oven for 1 hour. Makes 4 generous servings.

If you prefer a bit of crusty browning on your casserole, remove the cover the last 10 minutes of baking time.

MRS. PEALE'S ONION-BEEF-MACARONI CASSEROLE

1 cup macaroni
1½ pounds ground lean
  beef
1 envelope Lipton onion
  soup mix
1 tablespoon flour

1 8-ounce can tomato
  sauce
2 cups water
¼ cup grated Cheddar
  cheese

Heat oven to 400° F. Cook macaroni as package label directs. Drain it well. In a large skillet brown the meat, breaking it up with a fork as it cooks. Drain off any excess fat from the beef. Stir in the soup mix, flour, tomato sauce and water. Bring the mixture to a boil; reduce heat; cover and simmer for 5 minutes. Stir in macaroni. Turn into a 2-quart casserole. Sprinkle with cheese. Bake in preheated oven for 15 minutes. Makes 6 servings.

Mrs. Luisa Landi, known affectionately as "Nanna" to her children, grandchildren and friends, at ninety-one is our oldest celebrity. She lives with her daughter Sandra and her son-in-law Dr. Louis J. Camuti in Mount Vernon, New York. (Dr. Camuti, a veterinarian who specializes in cats, lists among his patients the former screen and TV personality, Rhubarb. Though over the conventional retirement age himself, he still works a twelve-hour day, making rounds from twelve noon to twelve midnight—"rounds" because Dr. Camuti feels it is less upsetting to all concerned to treat his little cat patients in their homes.)

Nanna's husband was the sculptor Sidardo Landi, whose bronze Redfield Monument is a landmark in Syracuse. Vivacious and tiny, she is admittedly the best cook in the family and still prepares most of the meals for the Camuti household. This menu is a family favorite.

Menu for a Camuti Family Get-Together

Boiled Beef
Torta di Zucchini*
Tossed Green Salad with Oil and Vinegar
Italian Bread   Sweet Butter
Spumoni
Nanna's Jelly Bars*
Coffee

TORTA DI ZUCCHINI

*2 pounds zucchini (long
and thin is best)*
2 tablespoons shortening
*2 medium-sized onions,
thinly sliced*
*1 1-pound can tomatoes,
coursely mushed (2 cups)*
*2 teaspoons chopped
parsley*
1 teaspoon salt

⅛ teaspoon pepper
¼ teaspoon dried orégano
*½ cup plus 2 tablespoons
fine bread crumbs*
*¼ cup grated Parmesan
cheese*
*¾ cup grated sharp Cheddar
cheese*
2 eggs, slightly beaten

Wash zucchini and cut it into ⅛-inch-thick round slices. Heat oven to 325° F. In a large skillet heat the shortening. Add onions and cook over medium heat just until they are soft and transparent. Add zucchini and cook for 5 to 7 minutes or until it is just beginning to be tender, turning it occasionally with a spatula to keep it from sticking to the pan. Add tomatoes, parsley, salt, pepper, orégano, the half cup of crumbs, Parmesan and Cheddar cheese. Stir in eggs. Grease an 11-inch pie plate or a 14-inch pizza pan or 2 8-inch pie plates. Coat the pan well with 1 tablespoon of the remaining crumbs. Pour in the zucchini mixture. Spread it out evenly. Sprinkle with the rest of the crumbs and bake in preheated oven for 1 hour and 15 minutes or until the *torta* is crisp and browned. Cool slightly and cut into wedges. Makes 8 servings.

For small-family use, cut all ingredients in half and prepare as directed. Bake in 1 8-inch pie plate. Makes 4 servings.

NANNA'S JELLY BARS

2 cups all-purpose flour
⅔ cup sugar
½ teaspoon baking powder
¼ teaspoon salt
¾ cup margarine (1½
  sticks)
1 large egg

2 teaspoons vanilla extract
  or 1 teaspoon each
  vanilla and lemon extract
½ cup raspberry or
  strawberry jelly
Confectioners' sugar

Heat oven to 350° F. Sift together flour, sugar, baking powder and salt. Cut in margarine, using a pastry blender or 2 forks, until the flour mixture resembles grains of rice. Blend in egg and extract. Form dough into a ball. Dough will be crumbly. (If it is too dry to hold together, sprinkle in just enough cold water to make the mixture hold together.) Divide the pastry into 3 equal parts. Shape each into a roll about 13 inches long. Place the rolls of pastry on ungreased cookie sheets. With the handle of a teaspoon make a deep groove down the center of each roll. Fill the depression with jelly. Bake in preheated oven for 15 to 20 minutes or until golden brown. Dust with confectioners' sugar. Cut *immediately* into diagonal strips about 1 inch wide. With a spatula remove bars to a wire rack to cool. Store in an airtight container. Makes about 3½ dozen.

Dr. Ancel Keys, Director of the School of Public Health at the University of Minnesota, contributed the following lighthearted but practical menu and recipes. Dr. Keys, well known for his research on heart disease and nutrition, author of the book *Eat Well and Stay Well,* gives credit to Mrs. Keys for the actual selection of both menu and recipes. His comment about suitable white wines is worth passing along. "You will note," he says, "that we have included sherry with the before-dinner dip and advised Pinot-Chardonnay to accompany the meal. Actually, many other dry white wines would do about as well—Rhine or Alsatian Riesling, a Soave or dry Orvieto from Italy, a good California Riesling, etc." This delightfully different menu is a fine one for relaxed entertaining, whether the budget is of prime importance or not.

Dr. and Mrs. Ancel Keys' Menu

Clam and Cottage Cheese Dip*
Corn Chips
Dry Sherry

Chafing-dish Garbanzos*
Baked Ham—Hot or Cold
Hard Rolls   Margarine
Chilled Pinot-Chardonnay
(or other dry white wine)
Leaf Lettuce Salad   Vinegar and Oil Dressing
Stuffed Baked Apples*

CLAM AND COTTAGE CHEESE DIP

*1 12-ounce carton
low-calorie cottage cheese
(labeled in some areas
as cottage cheese with
dressing, 2 per cent
butterfat)
¼ cup milk*

*1 8-ounce can minced
clams
Pinch salt
Few drops onion juice
Few grains garlic salt
(optional)*

Combine all ingredients in a blender. Blend at medium speed for 15 seconds. Dip is best when prepared in advance and refrigerated for several hours. Makes about 1½ cups dip.

CHAFING-DISH GARBANZOS

(From Dr. Keys' book, *The Benevolent Bean*)

3 tablespoons vegetable oil	1 7½-ounce can peeled
2 medium-sized onions,	solid-pack tomatoes
chopped	2 15-ounce cans garbanzos
1 green pepper, seeded	(chick-peas)
and diced	1 teaspoon salt
1 clove garlic (optional)	Pinch orégano

Heat oil in a chafing dish.[3] Add onion and green pepper and cook over low heat, stirring occasionally, until onion is transparent. Add garlic, if used, tomatoes, *garbanzos,* salt and orégano. Simmer, stirring occasionally, for 15 minutes, or until most of the liquid is absorbed. Remove the garlic. Makes 4 to 6 servings.

[3] If preferred, use an electric fry-pan or a heavy skillet over direct low heat.

STUFFED BAKED APPLES

4 large baking apples	¼ cup seedless raisins
2 walnuts	4 tablespoons sugar

Heat oven to 375° F. Core apples and place them in a baking dish. Break the walnut meats into pieces; mix with raisins and use the mixture to fill the centers of the apples. Add 1 tablespoon of sugar to the center and top of each apple. Cover the bottom of the baking dish with about ½ inch of water. Bake in preheated oven for 30 minutes or until apples are fork-tender, basting 3 or 4 times during baking. Chill before serving. Makes 4 servings.

Pearl S. Buck, as her fans know, lived for many years in China—the Old China which was the inspiration for her best seller *The Good Earth,* as well as for many other stories. Her books have brought her such coveted awards as the Pulitzer prize, awarded in 1932, and the Nobel Prize in Literature, received in 1938. Needy children have always touched Miss Buck's heart, and now at her country home in Pennsylvania she gives a loving home to many such children who badly need security and a family to belong to.

Pearl S. Buck's Menu

Sweet-Sour Spareribs*
Chinese-style Fresh Asparagus*
Melba Toast
Canned Purple Plums
Almond Cookies
Tea

SWEET-SOUR SPARERIBS

2½ *pounds spareribs*
2 *cups water*
4 *tablespoons soy sauce*
1 *teaspoon salt*
3 *tablespoons sugar*
3 *tablespoons vinegar*

2 *teaspoons cornstarch*
½ *cup water*
2 *tablespoons sherry*
1 *teaspoon fresh scraped*
   ginger root[4]

Cut the ribs into separate pieces. Bring the 2 cups water, soy sauce and salt to a boil in a large saucepan with tight-fitting cover. Add spareribs; cover and cook over medium heat for 1 hour, adding more water, if necessary, to keep ribs from sticking. Remove cover; turn heat high until moisture is absorbed. Blend sugar, vinegar, cornstarch, the remaining half cup of water and sherry to a smooth paste. Add ginger root and stir the mixture into the spareribs in the pan. Cook over low heat, stirring constantly, until the gravy is smooth, clear and bubbling. Makes 4 generous servings.

[4] Fresh ginger can be purchased in most oriental food stores.

CHINESE-STYLE FRESH ASPARAGUS

1½ to 2 pounds fresh
    asparagus
⅓ cup butter or margarine
⅓ cup water

¼ teaspoon salt
¼ teaspoon monosodium
    glutamate
Dash pepper

Break off the tough ends of the asparagus stalks. Wash the tips with cold, running water, scrubbing them gently, if necessary, with a soft brush to remove grit. With a vegetable parer, scrape the skin and scales from the lower part of the stalk. Slice the stalks on the diagonal, making bias slices about ½ inch long. In a large skillet with a tight-fitting cover heat the butter and water to a boil. Add the asparagus and remaining ingredients. Cook, covered, over high heat for 6 to 10 minutes, adding a little more water if necessary to keep asparagus from sticking to the pan. Asparagus should be fork-tender and the moisture should have all evaporated. Makes 4 generous servings.

Chapter Eleven

HELPFUL BOOKLETS
AND PAMPHLETS

It is a good idea to keep abreast of the progress being made concerning the health and welfare of retired people. You may want to order some of the following government bulletins for your own use or for a club reference library. To obtain any of them, write to the United States Government Printing Office, Division of Public Documents, Washington, D.C. 20402. Order each booklet by its title and catalog number. Enclose a check or money order in the amount of the price listed. Prices are given both for individual booklets and for quantities whenever this service is available.

Following the list of government publications, a few others, headed "Miscellaneous," cover areas of interest to those already enjoying their leisure years as well as to those who soon will be.

Government Social Security and Medicare Pamphlets

Are You Planning on Living the Rest of Your Life:
   Catalog No. FS 15.2:L 76.   30 cents

Benefits of Widows at Age 60 Under Social Security:
   Catalog No. FS 3.25/2:965/5.   5 cents each
                                     $2.50 per 100

Casework Service in Public Assistance Medical Care:
   Catalog No. FS 14.202:M 46/2.   35 cents

Changes in Social Security Disability Benefits:
Catalog No. FS 3.25/2:965/8.   5 cents

Provisions for Medical and Remedial Care:
Catalog No. FS 14.213:49. $1.25

Provisions for Social Services:
Catalog No. FS 14.213:53. $1.00

Health Insurance for People 65 and Older. A Brief Explanation of "Medicare":
Catalog No. FS 3.35:883.   10 cents
                                    $5.00 per 100

If You Become Disabled:
Catalog No. FS 3.35:29/13.   10 cents
                                    $6.50 per 100

If You Work While You Get Social Security Payments:
Catalog No. FS 3.35:23/15.   10 cents
                                    $5.00 per 100

Planning for the Later Years:
Catalog No. FS 3.2:P 69/965.   35 cents

Protective Services for Older Persons:
Catalog No. FS 14.213:54.   20 cents

Social Security Amendments, 1965:
Catalog FS 3.25/2:965/1/rev. 2.   10 cents
                                      $5.00 per 100

Social Security Cash Benefits, How to Estimate the Amount, How to Earn Them, How Much Credit You Need:
Catalog No. FS 3.35:855/10.   10 cents
                                   $5.00 per 100

Social Security for Clergymen under the 1965 Amendments:
Catalog No. FS 3.25/2:965/12.   5 cents
                                     $2.50 per 100

Social Security for Physicians:
Catalog No. FS 3.25/2:965/7.   10 cents
                                    $5.00 per 100

Social Security for Servicemen and Veterans:
Catalog No. FS 3.25:31a/5.   5 cents
                               $5.00 per 100

Special Information for Self-Employed Farmers:
Catalog No. FS 3.35:25d/8.   5 cents each
                               $3.00 per 100

Special Information for Self-Employed People:
Catalog No. FS 3.25/2:966/1.   5 cents
                                 $3.00 per 100

Special Social Security Benefits for People 72 or Over (under a change made in the law in 1966):
Catalog No. FS 3.25/2:966/1.   5 cents
                                 $3.00 per 100

Government Nutrition and Food Booklets

Money-saving Main Dishes:
Catalog No. A 1.77:43/3.   20 cents

Facts About Nutrition:
Catalog No. FS 2.22:N 95.   15 cents

Eat to Live Better:
Catalog No. A 1.68:694.   5 cents

Food Guide for Older Folks:
Catalog No. A 1.77:17/6.   10 cents

Be a Good Shopper:
Catalog No. A 43:2:Sh7.   5 cents

Meat for Thrifty Meals:
Catalog No. A 1.77:27.   20 cents

The Food We Eat:
Catalog No. A 1.38:870/3.   10 cents

Miscellaneous Government Pamphlets

Part-time Employment for Older People:
   Catalog No. FS 14.11:K 41/2.   15 cents

Free-time Activities, Recreation,
   Volunteer Services,
   Citizen Participation:
   (order by name only)   30 cents

You, the Law and Retirement:
   Catalog No. FS 14.8:R 31.   No Charge

Miscellaneous Publications Other Than Government

Order the following five pamphlets from:
   The National Safety Council
   425 North Michigan Avenue
   Chicago, Illinois 60611

"Fail Safe" Leaflets: How to Prevent Burns No. 599.01
                      How to Prevent Cuts No. 599.02
                      How to Prevent Falls No. 599.03
   Individual copy, no charge. 50 copies, 39 cents.

Family Emergency Almanac:
   Individual copy, no charge. 50 copies, 22 cents.

Hazard Hunting:
   Individual copy, no charge. 50 copies, 84 cents.

Pocket Guide to First Aid:
   Individual copy, no charge. 50 copies, 79 cents.

Safety Hints for the Elderly:
   Individual copy, no charge. 50 copies, 34 cents.

Other Publications

Modern Maturity, published by the American Association of Retired Persons, is mailed every two months (six times a year) to all members. If you are not a member and wish to become one, write to:

AARP Membership Division
406 East Grand Avenue
Ojai, California 93023

Originally AARP was AART, or the American Association of Retired Teachers, but now it includes all who wish to join and are fifty-five years old or older. Membership dues per year are $2.00 for residents of the United States—$3.00 per year for those outside domestic United States mail limits. AARP members not only receive *Modern Maturity,* a magazine filled with pertinent information, but are also entitled to many other benefits, such as drugs at a substantial savings and AARP low-cost group travel in the United States, Europe and even around the world.

Planning Kitchens for Handicapped Homemakers, by Virginia Hart Wheeler, Kitchen Planning Consultant, The Institute of Physical Medicine and Rehabilitation. New York University Medical Center, 400 East 34th Street, New York, New York 10016. $2.00 per copy.

INDEX